Rescue Me!

By Bardi McLennan

Kennel Club Books·

EDITORIAL
Andrew DePrisco *Editor-in-Chief*
Peter Bauer *Managing Editor*
Amy Deputato *Senior Editor*
Jonathan Nigro *Editor*
Matt Strubel *Assistant Editor*

ART
Sherise Buhagiar *Graphic Layout*
Bill Jonas *Book Design*
Joanne Muzyka *Digital Art*

Copyright © 2007

Kennel Club Books®

A Division of BowTie, Inc.

40 Broad Street • Freehold, NJ • 07728 • USA

Cover photo: Cover dog Lucy was dumped at a shelter when her breeding days were over. Taken in by the Lincoln family as a foster dog, Lucy had other plans as she settled in and made herself right at home. The Lincolns now can't imagine their lives without their "Basset Hound queen." Photo by Tami Lincoln.

Thanks to the owners, photographers and rescue volunteers who submitted the photographs of the dogs featured in this book, including:

Megan Alexander
Christopher Appoldt
Russ Bain
Peter and Cindy Bauer
Helen Risom Belluschi
Mary Bloom
the Bonner family
Barbara Booth
the Brodie family
Kathy Brunner
George Burton
Anne Campbell
Jessica Carlson
Joan Cavanaugh
Lisina Ceresa
Justin Christian
Frank and GerriLynn
    Connors

Barbara Curtis
the Dahl family
the Daum family
Barbara Davis
Christopher Deputato
the Deputato family
Gerry and Marilyn
    Deucher
the Dossey family
the Faust family
Melissa Fenwick
Ruth Fenwick
Anna Mae and Bill Flynn
Marilyn and Lowell
    Henderson
Amy Hendrickson
Laura Holum
the Keane family

Lex Kelly
Patrick and Andrea Kelly
the Kimmel family
Kim and Scott Kline
Victor LaBruna
Phillip Lang
Jackie Laverne
the Lazarus family
Jose and Lynda
    Maldonado
Susan Marino
the Martinez family
the McBride family
Lee McMenimen
Connie Millard
Deborah Miller
Gale Ann Morris
Sarah Muir

the Nagy family
the Nigro family
the O'Neill family
Ann Ottavio
the Parker family
Keri Perez
the Peragino family
Lanelle Rachel
Walter Raps and Evelyn
    Ackley-Raps
Geula Resnick
the Rodriguez family
Timothy and Stephanie
    Rollins
Barry Rosen
Cathe Ross
Lee'Or Rutenberg
Lynn Schmitt

Hilary Scull
Stephen and Sara Seals
Jaimie Sherburne
Snootydog.com
Walter Staab
Deborah Stevenson
April Stickel
Mary Anne Sullivan
Donyale Testa
Tien Tran Photography
Cathy Toft
Liza Wallis
Diane Walsh
Riannon Walsh
the Wilkins family
the Wilson family
Joyce Yaccarino
John W. Yeomans

Library of Congress Cataloging-in-Publication Data
McLennan, Bardi, 1926-
    Rescue me / by Bardi McLennan.
        p. cm.
    Includes index.
    ISBN-13: 978-1-59378-666-3
    ISBN-10: 1-59378-666-2
    1. Dogs. 2. Dog adoption. 3. Animal shelters. I. Title.
SF427.M4736 2007
636.7--dc22
                        2007006869

Printed and bound in Singapore

10 9 8 7 6 5 4 3 2 1

Contents

Bella **(LEFT)** ended up in a shelter after her owner died, while Brisco **(RIGHT)** spent two months in a shelter after being picked up as a stray. These two hound mixes were adopted by a family active in hound rescue and are very devoted "siblings"; in fact, due to their similar looks, they are often thought to be related.

CHAPTER 1

The Reality of Dog Rescue

Rescue. The word conjures up all of the good things that people do in this world in order to save something of value, from recycling newspaper to preserving historical monuments to saving a life. Did you know that, in addition to people who are trained to save lives, there are canines who are specially trained to assist in the rescue of humans? Search and rescue (SAR) dogs, as they are officially known, are on the scene of disasters worldwide. These include natural catastrophes such as hurricanes and avalanches as well as man-made ones such as collapsed buildings and war zones. Search and rescue dogs are also called upon to locate people who have been abducted or have become lost. These highly trained "super dogs" are the rescuers, definitely not the ones in need of being rescued.

However, for many other dogs, the need for rescue is real. In this case, it is the human who saves the dog's life. A dog may be stray, lost, abandoned, living with owners who can no longer care for him, living with abusive owners or on "death row" at a shelter; whatever the reason, this dog needs someone to rescue him, and soon. There are two essential parts to the reality of rescuing a dog. One is the person or family who takes the dog into his/their home. The other is all about the reality of the dog himself.

Rescued "siblings" Mario and Lucy are as comfortable as can be in their loving home. Chihuahua mix Mario was adopted from a town shelter and Pug mix Lucy came from an all-dog rescue.

has been bounced around from home to home and this is his third or fourth adoption. Perhaps you have no idea why this dog is currently without a home. While what you do know about the dog and his background will help the two of you adjust to each other, you should not worry about or speculate about the things in his past about which you don't know. The simple reality is that you've taken in this dog and now it is up to you to provide him with a good life.

The other part of rescue concerns, obviously, the dog. One or more times in his life he has had to adjust his behavior, language comprehension and routine to those of human strangers. He had a family (no matter who, what or where that family is or was) and now he does not (regardless of how or why); this has no doubt left the dog slightly confused. Now the reality is that the rescued dog has to unlearn many things that were his normal way of life and, at the same time, learn new things to fit into

The person taking in a rescued dog must first face and accept the fact that what this dog needs is a caring home, not people who dwell on what his life might have been like before. As the dog's new owner, perhaps you truly rescued him from cruelty or even death. Perhaps the dog your family, your lifestyle, your home and your routine. You, as the new owner, will need to cope with puzzling behavior and maybe even strange reactions to your everyday routine.

You are doing a great kindness in taking this dog into your home and family, but you are also acquiring a friend. It's a type of dog partnership unlike any other. Embarking on the ownership of a previously owned dog is unique and in many ways especially rewarding.

Adopting a rescued dog is not the same as selecting a puppy from a breeder and assuming all the joys (and problems) of raising a pup who grows up knowing only what you've taught him. (Okay, plus what he has taught you.) It's not the same as taking on an older dog from a near and dear relative who is now in a nursing home. It is not the same as acquiring an adult dog from the breeder who raised him. Whether you acquire your dog from a shelter or local dog pound or from a rescue organization, every

WHEN THE TIME IS RIGHT

If you have just lost a dog, it is generally considered best to wait a bit before getting another. It may be a lonely time for you, but no dog wants to come into a home where people are sad or where he is going to be constantly compared with the previous canine occupant. You are not replacing the dog you lost, as no dog can be "replaced." Each one comes in on his own four feet, with a different personality to make his own contributions to your life and your store of memories.

Begin your search for a new pal when the time is right, when you are thinking less about how much you miss the dog who is no longer with you and more about the need to find, know, appreciate and share your life with a new dog.

rescue adoption is unique. We will discuss the different types of adoption so that you can make yours a success.

Each rescued dog is an individual, starting out a new life with new people. You may have been given some background on the dog, or you may never know anything about the dog's life prior to his coming home with you. It is so easy, and such a common mistake, for dog-adopting good Samaritans to

At just two and a half months old, Italian Greyhound Cricket, a.k.a. "CeCe," was turned into a Pennsylvania rescue that usually deals with retired racing Greyhounds. She certainly held her own with the "big dogs" in her foster home and was adopted by an IG-loving couple.

of rescue and shelter dogs come from fairly ordinary circumstances.

Please promise yourself that you won't dwell on aspects of past abuse or mistreatment even if you know any portion of them to be true. Any pooch worth his weight in dog biscuits will gaze into your face while you recount these sad, heart-rending tales and seem to agree with your every word. He'll probably look more woebegone as you go on...and no doubt head for the cookie jar when you pause for breath!

Of course, a dog with a history of abuse will require a certain type of sensitivity on your part as you help him adjust to life in a caring home, but you didn't rescue this dog to feel sorry for him or to dwell on his past. You

assume that this "poor dog" had a horrible life, was starved, abandoned, mistreated, abused...well, you get the idea. While it is true that some canine adoptees suffered previous mistreatment, the majority rescued him so that you could give him a second chance at life and because you wanted the special bond that comes from the companionship of a canine friend. Concentrate on all of the positive things you need to do now in order to form the bond that will make you and the dog a team with happy days ahead.

OPT TO ADOPT

As someone looking to rescue a dog through adoption, you have several options. You can rescue a dog directly by visiting local shelters. You can research local all-dog rescue groups, which take in dogs of mixed and pure ancestry, to find out what dogs are available and learn about their adoption procedures. If you have a specific breed in mind, you can look for purebred rescue organizations, which are a wonderful option for purebred fanciers who like the idea of adopting rather than buying a dog. Most rescue groups have websites on which they list their adoptable dogs and often have online adoption applications to get the ball rolling. By adopting a dog in any of these ways, you are certainly rescuing that dog and contributing to the rescue effort at large by freeing up a space in a shelter or foster home for another dog who needs it.

LEFT: Italian Greyhound Rocky was adopted by the same couple who adopted Cricket (facing page).
ABOVE: Adopted from a high-kill shelter, Rottweiler mix Hannah now enjoys plenty of love and chew toys at home.

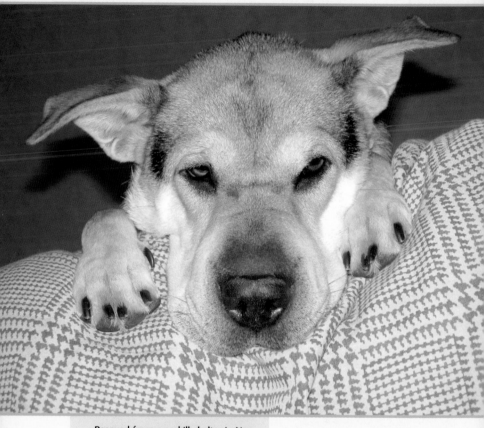

Rescued from a no-kill shelter in New York, Mosley now lives in her forever home in New Jersey. A Shar-Pei/German Shepherd mix, Mosley loves going to the beach with her family, keeping a watchful eye on her two human sisters and boisterously alerting everyone to the appearance of a pesky chipmunk.

CHAPTER 2

The Route to Rescue

GIVING UP ON THE DOG

Apart from an owner's giving up his dog due to a circumstance (e.g., death in the family, divorce, move to incompatible quarters), the most frequent reason for a dog's going into any rescue system or shelter is undesirable behavior. Unfortunately, this reason is often given even when the dog's behavior is perfectly normal canine behavior. This could mean a typical breed-specific behavior; for example, the owner didn't take it seriously when told, "This breed has a high energy level and needs lots of exercise." Or, "This breed likes to bark." Or, "This dog is not good with children under the age of five" Or, "This dog does shed." For a shelter dog of unknown background, the owner was probably advised that the dog might not be already housebroken or obedience-trained and that the owner will need to work with the dog on these things. At the time of the adoption, the overconfident new owner, excited by the prospect of his new canine companion, answered, "Oh, that's okay. I understand. I can handle that," only to find out later that he couldn't.

OTHER REASONS FOR OWNER SURRENDER

A potential dog owner may have specific issues, such as allergies, that affect his choice when deciding on a dog. When trying to select a dog that will be a good match, he may be told that certain

When Annie's owner passed away, a relative surrendered this sweet 13-year-old mixed-breed girl to a Yorkie rescue. She was adopted by a family and joined their two other rescue dogs. Her mom says, "She will have the best remaining years of her life."

people's allergies. It's also possible that someone in the family may develop an allergic reaction to the dog. Sadly, an allergic reaction can be primarily due to inadequate or improper grooming of the dog, but owners don't always listen to advice on how to reduce allergens in the home and instead look to give up the dog. Dogs that don't shed still require brushing, combing, clipping and bathing.

Speaking of grooming, this is another excuse for giving up on a dog. The new owner was told that the dog must be brushed and combed out at least once a week. However, after the novelty wore off, the weekly grooming sessions became a chore and suddenly there was no longer any time to keep up with the dog's grooming needs. Or perhaps the costs of professional grooming became too much for the owner to afford. Either way, the owner no longer wants to deal with the dog's upkeep and, as a result, looks to get rid of the dog.

breeds are hypoallergenic and therefore good choices for people with allergies. Any of the three sizes of Poodle, the Bichon Frise and some of the terriers are among the breeds often recommended, simply because they don't shed. However, these dogs still can end up in rescue because even a non-shedding dog can aggravate some

"Lack of time" is a reason right up there at the top of the list for someone's giving up his dog. Dogs are time-consuming. They cannot look after themselves or prepare their own meals. Dogs are "pack" animals that require the company of their leaders (humans). Left too much on their own without meaningful activity, dogs become destructive. Admittedly, people's lifestyles do change and too often people don't make adjustments to make sure that their dogs still fit into their lives. This is a sad reflection of our "easy come, easy go" society and the sort of careless reasoning that canine rescuers and shelter volunteers must deal with all too often.

On a similar note, owners sometimes find that a dog's health issues or changes that occur as the dog ages become more than they can or want to deal with. Such "special needs" dogs are often turned over by their owners; special needs include such things as loss of sight or hearing, loss of a leg or health problems that require close veterinary supervision. Adopting such a dog may simply mean knowing how to administer pills or eye drops or being able to maintain the dog on a special diet. These dogs can lead amazingly normal lives given the necessary extra attention.

After being rescued from a kill shelter, lucky girl Baby became a treasured member of her forever family.

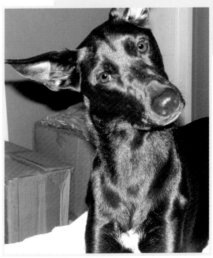

After being surrendered by her owners to an all-dog rescue, Lucy was adopted and now has sweet dreams in her forever home, which includes another rescued dog and two rescued cats.

Sadly, these dogs are often surrendered by their owners because the owners are no longer able to cope with the situation, either emotionally or financially.

Unfortunately, it's not always a matter of health. For example, an owner may give up an older dog who has become incontinent in old age. It's sad to hear about an owner who would give up an older dog that he's owned for the dog's entire life instead of making adjustments to accommodate the dog's needs in old age. In these cases, a "special needs" dog may just be very old and only in need of a quiet loving home with understanding care.

Priority is often given to adoption applicants who are willing and able to take on a dog with special needs. There are dogs of pure and mixed breeds in rescue groups and shelters all over the country who have disabilities or who require ongoing medical attention, but can live happily with the right owners and the right care. However, any dog that is found to be suffering or terminally ill is humanely put down by a veterinarian, often with one of those wonderful rescue volunteers offering words of comfort and soothing strokes up to the end. And no doubt shedding a tear for a dog he never knew.

WHERE DOES THE DOG GO?

When an owner has come to the decision that he is going to surrender his dog, what happens to the dog? In some cases, the owner and dog are fortunate to have a friend or family member offer to take the dog. However, more often the owner must turn to an outside source for help.

When buying a purebred dog, the owner needs to listen to advice about what to expect with that breed. For example, certain breeds,

Black and Tan Coonhound Winston started out in a North Carolina kill shelter, was taken in by breed rescue, was fostered in New Jersey and found his forever family in upstate New York.

ranging from the retrievers and some of the larger hounds and terriers down to several of the tiny toy breeds, remain in adolescence for their first few years. Some individual dogs of these breeds never outgrow this "teenage" stage. While this is completely normal, sometimes owners no longer enjoy or can cope with their dog's extended puppyhood and they look to give up the dog.

If the dog is a purebred that was bought from a reputable breeder, the breeder hopefully will be able to take the dog back, although this is not always possible. If the breeder cannot take the dog back for some verifiable reason, or if the purebred dog was not purchased from a breeder, the next step is breed rescue, which means a rescue organization dedicated to helping

Monroe was pulled from a rural shelter on his final day before euthanasia. He and other lucky dogs from the same shelter were transported to foster homes, and Monroe now enjoys his life with a loving new owner, a rescued German Shepherd and an adopted cat.

SURRENDERING A PUREBRED DOG

The person thinking about giving up his purebred dog should first contact the breeder from whom he bought the dog. Good breeders, especially those affiliated with breed clubs, usually pledge to take back dogs that they've bred at any time in the dogs' lives. However, there are situations in which this is not possible, as well as situations in which a purebred dog was obtained from a source that will not take the dog back. If your breeder cannot accept the dog back, he should work with you to find a breed rescue group who can take the dog. If your dog came from a source that will not help you, it will be up to you to contact a breed rescue representative or breed club member directly to find out where to start. In many breeds it is even possible to begin the process online by visiting the national breed club's website. Information on national breed clubs for the breeds recognized by the American Kennel Club can be found at www.akc.org.

Almost every national breed club spells out, most often in a Code of Ethics signed by breeder-members, that the breeder must take back, without a time limitation, any dogs they have sold. Therefore, if you contact the club first, you'll be asked right off the bat if your dog was purchased from a breeder who is a club member. If your answer is yes, the next question will be whether or not you have contacted the breeder about the situation. If there is a valid reason (and certainly there are some) why the breeder cannot take the dog back, the rescue group will take over. Usually once a dog is accepted into a rescue program, he is placed in a foster home while awaiting adoption. A rescue volunteer will lead you through the surrender process and will gather as much information about the dog and his background as possible. This enables the rescue group to place your dog into an appropriate foster home and to adopt him into the best possible permanent home.

and rehoming dogs of that particular breed. In addition to taking in owner-surrendered dogs, purebred rescue groups also spend a lot of time, money and effort rescuing "problem" dogs that were originally purchased from sources that do not take their dogs back regardless of the problem. Some purebred rescuers also rescue dogs of their breed that end up in animal shelters and pounds.

If the dog is a mixed breed, an owner should reach out to a rescue group that takes in all types of

When Mia's owner contacted a Pennsylvania rescuer about adopting a Yorkshire Terrier, the rescuer suggested that she consider Mia instead, a senior Chihuahua/terrier mix who she said had "the most beautiful soul." After taking her home, Mia's owner also discovered her dog's taste in fashion.

volunteers as they await adoption and also do in-depth screening of potential adopters. This offers assurance that your dog will be placed in a good home, something you can't be too sure about if you give your dog to the first person who answers an ad in the paper.

One obstacle you may encounter in reaching out to rescue groups is that they are unable to take your dog because they are full to capacity. Rescues are contacted very frequently by owners and shelters who ask for their help, so space limitations are usually a factor. Rescue groups rarely have physical facilities for housing dogs and thus rely on a network of volunteers to provide foster homes for the dogs up for adoption.

Dogs often end up in animal shelters when their owners either don't know about rescue groups, don't

dogs. While there are all-breed rescues that take in any type of purebred, there are also plenty of rescue groups that take in any kind of dog, mixed and purebred alike.

Reaching out to rescue groups, purebred or all-dog, is definitely the best option for someone looking to surrender his dog, as these groups keep the dogs in foster homes with caring take the time to reach out to rescue groups, cannot hold on to their dogs while waiting for a rescue to have open space or cannot find friends, family members or another trusted source to take the dogs. Shelters range from very good to those that hardly meet minimum standards, but any shelter environment can be quite confusing to a dog who has always lived in a home. It's also very important that owners are well aware of a shelter's policy before dropping off the dog. A no-kill shelter that actively promotes adoption usually has a high success rate in finding good homes for the dogs in their care. On the flip side, there are many shelters with high kill rates. No caring

owner would want to turn his dog over to a shelter that will euthanize the dog in a week if he is not adopted. Sadly, though, not all dogs are owned by caring owners.

LEFT TO RIGHT: Buster, Brewster and Sandman were brought in from the streets of Miami by a rescue group. After some time at the rescue's shelter facility, where they regained their health and confidence, the three dogs were adopted by the same family and are loved and well-adjusted companions—proud to be "Pure Mutts."

Enjoying the Northeastern winter is Beagle mix Genie, a confident city girl who was adopted from a shelter at nine months of age.

CHAPTER 3

Shelter Adoption

There are dogs and puppies available for adoption from your local town- or county-operated animal shelters and dog pounds. Dogs end up in shelters and pounds when they are either turned over by their owners or picked up by animal-control officers if they are stray or have become lost. These municipally run facilities must abide by local ordinances and state legislation, which means that some have a "no-kill" policy, while others are only allowed to keep dogs for a specified number of days. For example, some high-kill shelters have a holding period of a week or less for lost or stray dogs, after which time the dogs become available for adoption but also can be euthanized at any time. The holding period is often less for owner-surrendered dogs, as it is not necessary to give the owners time to reclaim them. Other shelters have a no-kill policy, which means that, after the specified holding period, dogs are available for adoption and can stay at the shelter until they are adopted. Some exceptions to the no-kill policy would be for aggressive or terminally ill dogs, which are humanely put down. In other instances, if a dog remains at the shelter for too long, he may start to develop behaviors that make him unsuitable for adoption. With both kill and no-kill facilities, dogs may be euthanized to make room for new dogs when the shelters are full. So even the no-kill shelters cannot adhere to a completely no-kill policy unless they are privately run and privately funded shelters that set their own rules and regulations.

Zack loves Mr. Bear, but not as much as he loves the caring owners who adopted him from a local shelter.

Dogs are rescued from shelters when they are either pulled by rescue groups or adopted directly by new owners. In the situation of high-kill shelters, dogs truly are rescued from death row when they get out. Other dogs have more time, but even in the best of shelters it's always a happy occasion when a dog can go to a good new home.

PROS AND CONS

The actual process of adopting a dog from a shelter or pound is usually not very complicated. The better shelters will have adoption applications and evaluation processes, while other shelters do little to no screening of potential owners. Acquiring a dog from the latter type of shelter involves very little effort and not much money.

Some shelters are large facilities with a professional staff that includes veterinarians, vet techs and even dog trainers. Others are quite small and, in addition, may be inadequately funded and thus can only provide very basic food and shelter. No matter how many animal shelters or dog pounds there are in this country, there are always many thousands more homeless dogs—purebred and mixed—than these facilities can accommodate.

Even with a better shelter, it will likely be more economical than adopting from a rescue group. Adopting from a shelter can be a wonderfully rewarding experience and can provide a deserving dog with a new chance at a good home. That being said, shelter adoption has its cons, too.

Unless the dog adapts to his new environment and family, he is likely to be caught up in a recycling scenario. When a dog is returned to the shelter, regardless of the reason, it presents problems for the poor dog, whose trust in people begins to run pretty thin. It also presents difficulties for the shelter, as a major problem faced by shelters is a lack of space. No matter how large the shelter, there are always more dogs than space. It is also a problem for the person who wanted to give the dog a good home but ran into unforeseen obstacles. He may never

have considered that taking on an adult dog would require all of the patience associated with training a young puppy. He fell for the "take me" pleading eyes and the wagging tail of a dog just hoping to be given another chance. Later, he realizes that he was not prepared for any dog, adult or puppy.

A dog that costs little or nothing may, to some people,

Adopted by two families that are close friends, former shelter dogs Mario **(LEFT)** and Bella **(RIGHT)** get together often for doggie playdates and have become the best of friends just like their humans.

SHELTER STATISTICS

While there are over 5,000 community animal shelters in the US, there is no national organization overseeing how they are run. The terms used, such as "humane," "animal guardian" or "welfare," are purely generic and are not a guarantee of anything pertaining to the dogs, their housing or their care.

Due to a lack of standardized record-keeping, the following statistics are only close estimates. They indicate that of the eight to ten million animals taken in by shelters annually, roughly 60% of the dogs are euthanized. Of the balance, there is a 20% return rate for medical or behavioral problems. Lost and found dogs don't fare much better. Only 15 to 20% of lost dogs that are found ever get back with their owners. Most of those lucky ones go back home due to the dogs' having proper ID tags, tattoos or microchips. As standard good practice, every dog should be given the security of a tattoo or microchip, neither of which can be lost or removed.

Statistics are from the National Council on Pet Population Study and Policy (NCPPSP), which is a coalition of animal-related organizations, and based on estimates from the American Society for the Prevention of Cruelty to Animals (ASPCA) and American Veterinary Medical Association (AVMA).

be worth little or nothing. The dog then gets little or no medical care and little or no proper training. When the owner tires of the dog for any reason, the dog is dropped off back at the shelter. That's the "easy come, easy go" way and it is bad…bad for the dog, that is. Not all shelters have a friendly "revolving door" policy. In many cases returned dogs are only given a few days or may even be put down right away.

On a good note, the fact that adopting a shelter dog usually requires only a small investment means that someone who cannot afford to pay a lot for a dog is still able to have the companionship of a dog. However, we're then back to the possibility of more things piling up on the bad side. If the person cannot afford decent dog food and basic veterinary care, then this dog, too, will end up back at the shelter.

Still another tragedy waiting to happen is the dog that is chosen for all the wrong reasons. We come back to that mistaken belief that all dogs ending up in shelters were abused, beaten, abandoned and starved. Most were not! Animals have a way of pulling at our heartstrings.

Feeling overly sorry for the poor, pathetic, cringing creature in a noisy, barren kennel is not sufficient reason to take him home. Remind yourself that the dog that walks out the door with you is counting on you to be his caretaker and trustworthy friend every single day for the rest of his life… that can be the next ten years or even longer.

On the flip side of the shy and scared dog is the dog that is jumping all over the place. You want to take him home because you think he's "stir-crazy" and only trying to escape his current imprisonment. That's what it may look like to you at the time. Only later will you come to your senses and realize that the dog is a wound-up bundle of non-stop excess energy—and you live not on a 200-acre cattle ranch but in an apartment on a busy city street!

Another error is when a potential adopter figures, "If it looks somewhat like a Pointer, it must be a Pointer." Mixed breeds can inherit the looks of one parent and the health and temperament of the other. What you see is not necessarily what you get. A friend who wanted a small dog adopted what she was told was a Beagle-mix puppy. When the dog grew much larger than expected, the owner couldn't keep him— a typical tale of a 90-pound pound puppy.

Adopted into her new family at age eight, Taffy now lives with two other rescue dogs. This smart girl always has kisses to share.

A dog at Dutchess County SPCA extends a paw to say hello.

When adopting from a dog pound, it may be an impulsive choice because you know that the dog you take a shine to today may be gone tomorrow. Unlike working with a rescue group or adopting from some private or no-kill shelters, where both you and the dog are evaluated at length and there is time to get to know the dog and make a decision, here you are confronted with numerous dogs, all saying "take me," and you alone must make the decision.

The animal-control officers in municipal pounds or shelters do not, and cannot, take these dogs home with them to evaluate the dogs' social skills or lack thereof. They may not be knowledgeable in canine behavior beyond the basics, partly because they are constantly dealing with so many different breeds and mixed breeds. Their jobs cover kennel work, keeping records of the dogs that come and go (or are put down) and dealing with the people who drop off and pick up the dogs. Plus, major functions of an animal-control officer are picking up lost or stray animals in the town and removing dogs that have been reported to them as being abused or kept in squalid or inhumane conditions.

With stray dogs or lost dogs who are not reclaimed by their owners, nothing is known about their backgrounds, personalities or temperaments. Shelter workers only get to know these dogs by observing them at the shelter. Some shelters do basic temperament testing before placing a dog up for adoption, although they are limited by the confines of the shelter environment. Unfortunately, though, other shelters do not keep dogs around for long enough to test them or even get to know them.

People who drop off a dog do not always tell the whole truth as to why they are giving it up, even when the shelter must document the information. It's hard for

BRING ON THE VOLUNTEERS

Good news for shelter dogs! In many towns, people with extensive experience in dogs—either with their own pets or through involvement in obedience training or therapy work—are volunteering to spend time with the shelter and pound dogs. They walk the dogs around the property, offer treats to encourage trust, spend time in interactive play and may even do some training. All the while they are providing companionship and attempting to get to know the dogs as best they can under the circumstances. In the process, volunteers can form a better idea as to what kind of home might be best for each dog. The shelter volunteers help not only the dogs, but also the would-be adopters, and they certainly take some of the load off the animal-control officers. We don't know if dogs are able to hope, but at least the one-on-one attention from and activity with the volunteers gives them some company and fun in an otherwise boring existence in the dog pound.

Shelters in some towns and communities have started after-school programs for children (who meet age requirements) to help care for the animals. Under good adult supervision, kids can help out in many ways: grooming, refilling water bowls, feeding, etc. Many are children who are not able to have a pet of their own, so the appreciation goes both ways. Plus, teaching the kids to be kind and caring with homeless animals extends into their own lives.

FACING PAGE: At Animal Haven shelter, which has several locations in New York, volunteers make sure that the animals are cared for, socialized and given good old-fashioned attention and petting.

people to admit that they are wrong. It is so much easier just to say that the dog "misbehaves" than to admit that they never trained the dog or to tell the shelter workers, "He killed two of our five cats, and I guess we forgot to tell you about having cats when we got the dog from you in the first place."

In the worst-case scenario, the dog is dropped off without the owner's informing the shelter officials about serious behavioral problems. These can range from a hard-to-manage dog with an assertive or domi- nant personality to an actively aggressive dog that has actually bitten or

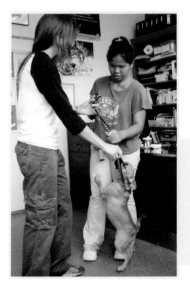

LEFT: An experienced Animal Haven volunteer helps a new volunteer get started. **ABOVE:** Shelters appreciate donations of crates, blankets, toys and other items to help make the animals comfortable.

Temperament testing at the Humane Society of New York. Bill Berloni evaluates how the dog reacts to being put in a submissive position.

The dog is tested to see if he knows any commands and is also offered a toy to see if he exhibits possessive behavior.

Temperament testing also gauges how a dog gets along with other dogs; this is important for adopters who already own dogs.

It's a brave cat who is picked for the job of "feline-compatibility tester."

An ASK volunteer's job is time-consuming and physically demanding, but the rewards far outweigh the effort.

Linda and her crew rely on donations, organization and teamwork to get their jobs done.

LITTLE SHELTER'S COMMUNITY OUTREACH

In addition to providing care and a second chance for many homeless animals, the Little Shelter reaches out to members of its Long Island, New York community who need assistance caring for their pets. No matter how much they love their pets, people sometimes do not have the means to care for them properly with adequate food, veterinary care, shelter and the like. In looking for a way to help, Linda Klampfl attended a "Training Wheels" course taught by founder Sue Sternberg of Rondout Valley Animals for Adoption in upstate New York. Once certified in the program, Linda and her volunteers put it into practice in their own community.

Renamed the Animal Soup Kitchen on Wheels (ASK), this program provides food and equipment for pet owners. Linda and her ASK team load up their van and head into the poorer neighborhoods, visiting the homes of owners who have reached out for help. They bring bags of food, collars, leashes, tie-outs and even dog houses and straw for outdoor shelter, whatever is needed. The ASK volunteers will also transport pets to and from the veterinarian's office at no cost to the owner. An important facet of this is educating owners about spaying and neutering. If the owner agrees to have his pet altered, the ASK team will take care of the transportation and fees.

As news about the program spreads, mostly through word of mouth, more and more families reach out for help. Supplies and veterinary care demand much from the Little Shelter in time, manpower and funds, but the work is extremely rewarding, as people are able to keep and care for the pets that they love. Because of this, and because of the reduction in unplanned litters due to spaying and neutering, another positive result is a decrease in the number of animals being turned over to shelters. The ASK team also educates the public through programs in local schools to teach children about responsible pet ownership.

"I really believe we have to bring the shelter to impoverished pet owners before they turn their pets into the shelter out of frustration," says Linda Klampfl, "The Little Shelter van brings much-needed supplies and the Training Wheels team brings the caring and education necessary to turn an unsafe environment into a loving and permanent adoptive home."

You can find out more about the ASK program and read Linda's frequent updates on what the team is doing by visiting the shelter's website at www.littleshelter.com and clicking on the Animal Soup Kitchen on Wheels link.

Volunteers brought this dog an igloo-type doghouse and they regularly bring him food and fresh straw.

A pet dog shows his gratitude for the ASK team's help.

In addition to interacting with the animals, shelter staff and volunteers are responsible for keeping the kennels and all areas clean.

attacked another dog or person. The animal-control workers may not witness the behavior if it only occurs under specific circumstances. Too often, children are the victims of dog aggression. It may have been the kids who were at fault, teasing or playing too roughly with the dog, but it's tough for parents to admit that. They then take the easy way out and get rid of the dog, saying only that they can't make him behave.

Any dog known to be aggressive when brought to a shelter—private or municipal—is euthanized. This is exactly what happens in the case of a rescue group, too. Such a dog is potentially dangerous and would not be put up for adoption by any reputable rescue organization. Canine aggression ranges from a noisy barking/growling reaction directed at another dog all the way to a vicious attack, with or without warning, on a person or another animal.

No shelter or rescue can take a chance with a dog's exhibiting any form of aggressive behavior. But if they aren't made aware of the aggression, and it doesn't surface at the shelter, the dog could be passed on to another family. It's a sad and potentially dangerous situation.

The most common reasons for giving a dog to a pound or shelter are the easy excuses: "We're moving (can't take the dog)," or "I have personal problems (dog doesn't like my new boyfriend)," or "I can't afford the dog (dog food, vet bills, etc., cost too much)" or "I don't have enough time for the pet (better things to do)." Only very occasionally does the truth come out that the dog is being left at the shelter because he is sick and the owner cannot afford proper care or because he bites.

If you are about to adopt a pound or shelter dog, take a good long look and decide

Socialization time not only is fun but also helps the shelter workers get to know the dogs and assess their personalities.

ANGEL'S GATE
By Susan Marino

From the street, it looks like any other house on the block. Just ordinary New York suburbia. But this home is anything but ordinary. Angel's Gate is a first: more than just a privately run shelter, this is a one-of-a-kind residential hospice for animals that opened its doors to welcome its first animal companion over 13 years ago. Angel's Gate is my dream. I have created a place where all beings, human or animal, are accepted as they are. It is a place where differences are honored and accepted, not shunned and dismissed. If an animal is battered, damaged or dying, he finds a home here. Angel's Gate is truly a home—it is my home and theirs. My name is Susan Marino and I founded this paradise that I share with my life partner Victor LaBruna.

Angel's Gate's mission is to catch the animals that fall between the cracks. It is a refuge for animals with no one to care for them. The animals come from individuals, veterinarians, shelters and rescue groups. The animals that arrive at Angel's Gate are often defeated physically, spiritually and emotionally. We can never make up for the years of abuse and neglect that many of the animals have suffered, but we can give them a new home that exudes kindness and compassion. Animals come to Angel's Gate from all over the world for different reasons. Many of the animals have incurable or terminal diseases. Some have neurological problems or just are old and some are incontinent or paralyzed. But there is one undeniable common thread—each animal that comes to Angel's Gate is a teacher and is here to share his wisdom before he passes.

Angel's Gate flows with the rhythm of the day and no two days are exactly alike. Yes, the animals are dying, but today they are very much alive. Our day begins very early and often goes late into the night. Our goal for each day is to celebrate life and not take one moment for granted. I believe in the body's ability to heal; given a healthy diet and supplements and a loving environment, I have found that healing happens. We are frequently witness to many miracles.

We have many success stories here at Angel's Gate. There are quadriplegic animals who are now walking, diabetic cats who no longer need insulin and animals with cancer who have far exceeded their life expectancies, but the greatest success story we can offer here is death with dignity. Every animal passes surrounded by people who care. The animals have taught me to be present and that life is to be joyful even when it is ending. I have had the honor of being witness to many animals' leaving this life and moving on to whatever awaits them. But are they really gone? They are so much a part of the fabric of Angel's Gate.

Long after they are gone I feel them in the breeze on my face and smell them in the dew that glistens on the grass and see them in the glint of the late afternoon sun as it warms the tiles in the foyer. Angel's Gate has many guardian angels forever looking over it.

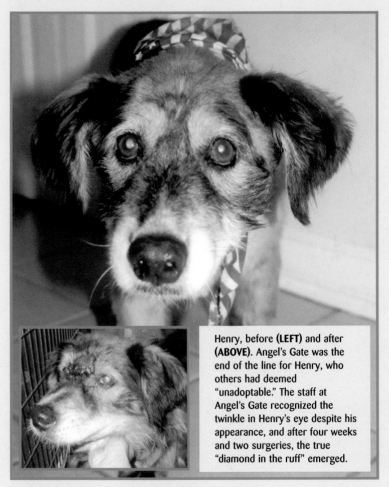

Henry, before **(LEFT)** and after **(ABOVE)**. Angel's Gate was the end of the line for Henry, who others had deemed "unadoptable." The staff at Angel's Gate recognized the twinkle in Henry's eye despite his appearance, and after four weeks and two surgeries, the true "diamond in the ruff" emerged.

The biggest perk of working or volunteering at a shelter? The doggie love, of course!

with your head, not just your heart. Talk to the shelter workers and volunteers about their adoption process. If this is a no-kill shelter or one that holds dogs for longer time periods, you may be able to visit the dog a few times to get to know him. In other shelters, dogs do not have much time, so you also will not have much time to make a decision. No matter what you pay in actual cash for a dog, it's only the amount of your own personal involvement that counts in the long run. Find out as much as you can about the dog you are considering, even if in the end it isn't much. "He's sweet" or "She's been really gentle" may be as much as you'll hear. When you walk out the door with that dog, you are starting from square one.

All dogs will have been vet-checked or at least given a round of vaccinations, and today most will have been spayed or neutered before adoption. No matter what you are told, take the dog (within 48 hours) to your own veterinarian with whatever health records you were given.

This dog is putting his life in your hands. Accept his trust and work with him gently and firmly. He will try to fit into your life with few, if any, problems. All behavioral problems need to be handled promptly or they will only get worse. There could be problems that you are only able to work out with the help of a professional trainer. Do it, and you'll be on your way to having a good bond with your canine friend.

PRIVATE ANIMAL SHELTERS

Throughout the country, privately run no-kill shelters and animal sanctuaries are cropping up, evoking interest and compassion from would-be adopters. Some of these are large facilities that can accommodate large

A good shelter will be clean and offer each dog his own adequate space.

numbers of animals, some specialize in taking care of special-needs animals, some operate to promote or publicize a specific point of view regarding animals, etc. In addition to donations, all are funded by anything from tag sales to philanthropic neighbors to large organizations, so they either operate on a shoestring or are relatively well endowed.

Private shelters operate like rescues, although the main difference is that they have physical facilities to house the animals. Private shelters often fill the gap when municipal pounds are either filled to capacity or without sufficient funds to maintain a healthy environment for the animals. Sometimes these shelters will step in when a large number of animals needs rescue due to things like a natural disaster, abuse or hoarding cases

or another rescue's shutting down and needing help placing their animals. These shelters rely on both volunteers and paid workers. In some cases they also work to promote proper pet care and training. Some are even involved in pet therapy, taking suitable dogs to visit schools for the blind, nursing homes or children's hospitals where canine contact is warmly appreciated.

Local legislation generally prohibits private shelters from picking up stray or reportedly abused dogs, since that is the paid work of animal-control officers. Therefore, the dogs usually arrive at private shelters directly from the people giving them up, at which time the workers try to get as much information as possible about the dogs. The workers in some private establishments are able to take dogs home with

This outgoing shelter dog is eager to check out everyone who passes by.

them for evaluation of social skills. Occasionally, volunteers who are qualified trainers, breeders or behaviorists are able to work with the dogs on the shelter grounds.

Private shelters occasionally hold open houses or other events to familiarize area residents with their facilities, how they function and the animals currently awaiting new homes. A shelter that is legally established as a not-for-profit organization will state that fact on all of their printed material, on their website and on the receipt you get for your donation. Your donation (which is your payment for the dog) is then tax-deductible. And like other canine rescue groups, private shelters are always grateful for extra donations.

A sign at Dutchess County SPCA welcomes visitors and invites them to meet the animals for adoption.

Shelter staff must keep detailed paperwork on each animal, including known history, medical records, notes on behavior and any other pertinent information.

When a Border Collie breeder became ill and had to place all of his dogs, a Border Collie rescue stepped in to help with the placements. Emmy Lou, as beautiful as she is talented, was adopted into a Border Collie-loving family who worked with her to develop her natural abilities. She regularly competes in agility trials and has won several titles, and herding training is next on her horizon.

CHAPTER 4

Purebred Rescue

Most purebred rescue groups take in dogs of their breed from all types of people and situations. This means that in addition to accepting dogs surrendered by their previous owners, they also often take in lost, stray or owner-relinquished dogs of their breed that turn up at shelters and dog pounds. Active, responsible purebred rescue volunteers should reach out to shelters in their area to make their presence and willingness to help known. That way, a shelter will know whom to contact when dogs of these breeds turn up in their facilities. A good line of communication and mutual cooperation are essential to a good shelter/rescue relationship. The advantage for the purebred dog is that its rescue group has specific knowledge of that breed and likely has many people waiting to adopt a dog of that breed. Rescues screen potential adopters to make sure that they have a home and lifestyle that are compatible with the needs of their particular breed.

When breed rescue volunteers work with shelters, they first verify that the dog is, as far as can be determined, of their specific breed. Shelter workers do their best to identify the dogs that come into their shelters but do not pretend to be breed experts. Ungroomed shaggy dogs that arrive at shelters are all too easily mistaken for the wrong breeds. Is it a black Standard Poodle or an ungroomed Kerry Blue Terrier? A large Shetland Sheepdog or a small Collie? Is it a big Maltese, a small Bichon Frise or a white Miniature Poodle?

Rescued Sheltie Rudy is ten years old and still going strong, bringing comfort to those who need it as a therapy dog.

A problem for rescue groups to deal with when taking on shelter dogs is finding out the dogs' backgrounds. When a dog is owner-surrendered, the rescue volunteers get as much information as they can from the owners. However, with a lost or stray dog that is picked up by an animal-control officer, brought to the shelter and not reclaimed by his owner, the dog's history is completely unknown. Unlike in *Cheers*, the chances are that nobody knows his name! In the situation of an owner's turning his dog over to a shelter, the owner may or may not give accurate and complete information on the dog. In any case, the shelter workers give the breed rescue volunteers as much information as they have, and the rescue volunteers have to fill in the dog's history one bit at a time. The rescue group will have a vet determine the dog's approximate age, if unknown, and do an exam to assess his health. The volunteers then delve into things like finding out how the dog reacts to people, other dogs, cats, kids, collars, etc. And that's just for starters. Let's look in more detail at how purebred rescue volunteers do it.

HOW BREED RESCUE GROUPS OPERATE

Most national breed clubs today are incorporated not-for-profit organizations, and their rescue groups operate under the aegis of those parent clubs. The rules and regulations for rescue and adoption may vary from club to club, but despite the differences, it's pretty much a level playing field for every-one—those surrendering dogs, the rescue volunteers and the adopters. If you look at a specific breed club's website for rescue informa-tion, you'll find that a breed with many dogs in rescue likely has a number of contacts listed, usually by region or state and often with more than one in the same region or state. Some of these contacts may be indi-viduals, while some may be regional rescue groups that operate under the auspices of the national club. Regional rescue groups often have their own websites where you can learn about their adop-tion procedures and dogs avail-able. Breeds with fewer dogs coming into

rescue may only list contact information for the particular person who is in charge of the national club's rescue efforts.

A frequent complaint from would-be adopters is not getting a reply when they e-mail, write or phone rescue contact people. Potential adopters must understand that these rescue workers

Rottweiler Maggie was rescued after being thrown out of a car onto an expressway in New York at the approximate age of nine. Her spirit undamaged, Maggie is a true goodwill ambassador for her breed; she loves to give and receive attention and affection and is wonderful around friends of all ages.

RESCUE BY NUMBER

The American Kennel Club's "top ten" (most popular) breeds also have the most rescue dogs to house and foster while they await new homes. This is a considerable expense when 1,000 or more dogs in a single breed are in the rescue system. When you hear of large numbers of a "popular" breed being in rescue, bear in mind that it's a small number compared with the many dogs of that breed maintained in loving homes.

Each month the American Kennel Club registers over 10,000 Labrador Retrievers, 4,000 German Shepherd Dogs, Golden Retrievers and Beagles, 3,000 Boxers and Dachshunds…and the list goes on. In addition to the breeds who consistently land in the AKC's top ten, there are breeds such as the American Pit Bull Terrier, the Greyhound, the Jack/Parson Russell Terrier and many of the coonhound breeds that are more commonly registered by the United Kennel Club, or not at all, and thus are also among the country's most numerous. It is no wonder that there are seldom enough volunteers to open their homes to the many dogs of these breeds in need of rescue.

are volunteers, most of them with day jobs and families that also take up their time. Further, funds are not always available for rescue groups to return long-distance calls, so

if you're calling out of your area and you reach an answering machine, don't expect a return call. Call again or find a local person to contact. There may also be a temporary problem with the website or a computer glitch, so do follow up if you do not get a reply to an e-mail you've sent. Keep in mind also that volunteers are sometimes overwhelmed by rescue work. Don't give up— keep trying!

To understand in more detail about how purebred rescue groups operate, let's look at some examples in particular breeds. We begin with the most popular dog in the country now, the Labrador Retriever, and the Golden Retriever, close behind in popularity. As a result of their large numbers, both breeds are frequently available for adoption through breed rescue groups. We will then look at a range of other breeds, some common and some relatively rare, but all with very active and dedicated rescue programs.

Labrador Retrievers

The Labrador Retriever Club, Inc. (LRC) Rescue Support Group is one of the largest purebred rescue organizations in the US. This is not surprising, considering that over 10,000 Labs are registered each month with the American Kennel Club. The LRC's rescue effort consists of a national network of rescue organizations that is divided regionally, often with more than one group operating in a single state. A national coordinator oversees this network of rescue groups, which spans the entire country. When you visit the LRC's website at www.thelabradorclub.com and visit the rescue section, you can search for member groups in your region and contact them individually. While there are seldom young puppies in rescue (true of almost all breeds), each region usually has a good number of dogs awaiting adoption.

Labrador rescue will not accept into their program any dog that bites. This policy is set forth for safety, and it is important for the applicants' peace of mind to know about it. Further, all of the rescue Labs are neutered or spayed before placement (this holds true for all purebred rescue groups). As is done by more

A rescued Lab doing what the breed was meant to do, out in the field with his owner.

and more of the breed rescue groups, adopted Labs are microchipped, for which there is a small fee that includes registration.

A potential adopter's suitability for taking on a Labrador is carefully assessed, with a realistic approach to all of the negatives and positives. There is the usual in-depth application form followed by a home visit by rescue volunteers once the application is approved. Volunteers want to see for themselves that the fencing really is adequate, that the home is suitable for a large dog and so forth.

When an eligible dog is available for an applicant, some of the Labrador rescue groups require the potential adopter(s) (every member of the family, including any dogs) to go to the foster volunteer's house to meet the rescue dog. If all goes well, there is still a further 24-hour waiting period. When it's a "go," the new owners are given a two-week trial period after which, if all goes well, the adoption is official.

Golden Retrievers

The Golden Retriever Club of America (GRCA), with about 4,000 dogs registered with the AKC monthly, has numerous regional rescue groups listed by state on its website, www.grca.org. Like several other rescue organizations, Golden rescues adhere to the rule of placing their dogs locally. A little less than half of the dogs turned over to Golden rescue are surrendered by their owners due to behavior issues resulting from the owners' lack of time for both sufficient training and exercise. Very few are turned in due to health problems, which is good to know. More than half of the rescue Goldens up for adoption are under four years of age.

Some of the adoption rules may vary slightly among the regional groups, but all put the dogs' safety foremost. For example, among the policies of Yankee Golden Retriever Rescue, which covers New England, is a restriction regarding "hidden" electric fence systems. In fact, applications from first-time dog owners who intend to use these fences will not be approved. Further, no dog is placed in a residential facility such as a nursing home, halfway house, etc. Dogs taken in as strays or with unknown backgrounds will not be placed in homes with young children. Another regional group, Delaware Valley Golden Retriever Rescue, Inc., which

WHAT ABOUT MIXED BREEDS?

Many people may think that the only option for adopting or surrendering a mixed-breed dog is the local shelter, but this is not true. There are many "all-dog" rescues out there; these are rescue groups that take in mixed breeds and purebreds of any breed. These groups operate in the same way as purebred rescues—the dogs that they take in are owner surrenders, shelter dogs in danger of euthanasia or even lost or stray dogs whose owners cannot be located. Dogs coming into rescue are checked by a vet, temperament tested and placed into foster homes. This is a better transition for the dog, who can become confused and stressed by life in a shelter when he is used to life as a family dog. Likewise, it also assures that the dog will stay safe until he is readopted. Even good no-kill shelters sometimes face situations in which euthanasia becomes inevitable, such as if the shelter becomes overcrowded. The benefit for adopters is that the foster family can give potential new owners a good idea of the dog's behavior, temperament and training, because they have been living with the dog and know how he has responded in a home setting.

Some of these all-dog rescues concentrate on helping specific groups of dogs or dogs with certain needs. You can find rescues for small dogs, blind or deaf dogs, certain types of dogs (hounds, herding dogs, bully breeds, etc., and mixes thereof), senior dogs, pregnant dogs and the list goes on. For example, have you ever wondered what happens to dogs who are training to become guide dogs, search dogs or service dogs and "flunk" their training? That's right—you probably will find a rescue group just for them! There also are groups that work with certain shelters, rescuing the dogs who are on "death row" and are running out of time.

A good rescue group has detailed policies and procedures for intake, foster homes, screening of potential adopters, volunteers and adoption. Whether dealing with purebred dogs, mixed-breed dogs or a combination of both, reputable rescues all have the same goal: to put the dogs' best interests first and to match them up with the most suitable forever homes.

Bullmastiff Ciara's foster mom decided to become her forever mom after just three days of fostering her. Zoe the cat formed an immediate bond with her new canine family member, who is a gentle and welcoming rescue ambassador to all of the foster dogs who share their home.

operates in New Jersey and eastern Pennsylvania, reports having rescued and placed over 1,600 dogs since 1993.

The regional clubs under the auspices of the GRCA's national rescue committee have excellent overall adoption procedures from application to home visit to trial period to finalizing the adoption. It's not a hurry-up job. The average wait for a rescued Golden Retriever can be up to five months. The dog waits for the right home and the applicant waits for the right dog. That's the key to any successful rescue.

Boxers

There are between 35,000 and 40,000 Boxers registered with the AKC each year, ranking it consistently in the AKC's top ten most popular breeds. The American Boxer Rescue Association (ABRA) is another of the large nation-wide purebred rescue organizations. ABRA has a rescue Code of Ethics for their affiliate members and associate members. They also have a detailed surrender contract that must be signed and dated by the person surrendering the dog and by the rescue volunteer. The white Boxer (not recognized by the AKC) and mixed breeds that are part Boxer are included in their rescue program.

This is another rescue organization with a primary concern about each group's placing dogs locally. When that is not possible, the dog goes to a member group elsewhere in the country where an adoption can be made locally. It is a very wise method, as it assures that help and support will be nearby to those who adopt the dogs. Visit American

Three happy families own these five rescue Boxer best friends: Rocky, Bean, Lia, Spirit and Jake, all adopted through a breed rescue. Each of these dog's lives was truly saved by rescue, and now they are all loved, wanted and truly content.

DOGGIE BLOOD DONORS

Adopters of rescue dogs in several breeds—Boxers and German Shepherd Dogs among them—are encouraged to have their dogs donate blood, which is a simple five-minute process. Like humans, the dogs are given treats afterwards. But unlike humans, dogs don't have a universal donor type. There are more than a dozen canine blood types, according to the director of the canine blood bank at the University of Pennsylvania, which sends around a blood mobile on collection days in the area. With canine surgery on the increase, these donors help the entire canine community.

Boxer Rescue Association online at www.americanboxer rescue.org.

Beagles

Consistently ranking in the AKC's top ten breeds, with over 40,000 dogs registered annually, the Beagle is a breed always in need of rescue. Part of the rescue problem is that a good number of Beagles are kept as hunting dogs and many end up in shelters and pounds when their hunting days are over, if they didn't perform up to their owners' expectations or if they break loose from the pack and run away. Fortunately, many of these dogs, despite having lived as outdoor dogs and being unaccustomed to the life of a pet, can adapt to being good family companions. Unfortunately, the dogs in need usually greatly outnumber the rescue space available, but Beagle rescuers are a very dedicated bunch, often doing last-minute saves when they are alerted to Beagles about to be euthanized. Between shelter dogs, owner-surrendered dogs and dogs from other circumstances, Beagle rescuers certainly have their hands full.

The Beagle Rescue Foundation of America (BRFOA) is not involved with fostering and adoptions but is a non-profit organization that helps Beagle rescue groups with funding. This assistance is greatly needed by the rescue groups, who rely on donations to house, feed, care for and provide veterinary attention to the dogs they take in. A link to BRFOA can be found on the National Beagle Club's site, http://clubs.akc.org/NBC, along with a listing of regional Beagle rescues.

Cocker Spaniels

The American Spaniel Club Foundation (ASCF) is another organization in which affiliate member groups must agree to the ASCF's rescue policy and sign a rescue Code of Ethics annually. Rules such as this protect everyone, especially the dogs. The ASCF's adoption procedure and rescue format are otherwise fairly typical. The American Spaniel Club's website, www.asc-cock erspaniel.org, has a rescue section with more information about their adoption process and regional groups across the country.

Collies

The Collie Club of America's (CCA) Committee for Welfare and Rescue is another large organization with regional offshoots, which can be found

at www.collieclubof america.org. One of them assigns all rescued dogs a special file number, sort of like a "rescue registration." The normal initial rescue routine is followed when a dog is taken into rescue: grooming and a vet check, after which time the dog (if

Rescue Collie Argyle, a cast member of *Chitty Chitty Bang Bang* on Broadway, takes a break between shows with handler Rob Cox.

LEFT: Through the patience, effort and determination of Babe's new owner, this rescued Collie emerged from an extremely fearful, nearly catatonic, state to become a valued family member and successful competitor in agility and other disciplines. **ABOVE:** Rescued cast members of Broadway's *Chitty Chitty Bang Bang* include a Beagle, a Cocker Spaniel, a Collie and a Cavalier King Charles Spaniel.

healthy) is spayed or neutered and then placed into a foster home for intensive evaluation.

When a placement is made, obedience training is strongly recommended to lay the groundwork for a good bond between the dog and his new family. A one-month adjustment period is offered by some of the CCA rescue groups, during which time a full refund is given if the dog is returned. That is considerably longer than the trial period granted by most rescue groups and offers good "insurance" for both the dogs and those adopting them.

Scottish Terriers

The rescue arm of the Scottish Terrier Club of America (http://clubs.akc.org/stca) has a large network of some 50 contacts, plus regional clubs and offshoots that operate independently. Most take in only purebred Scotties, although some will also rescue and place Scottie mixes. Scottie rescuers are admirably upfront in explaining why someone might not be the right person for the breed. For example, they point out that the Scottie needs professional grooming every six to eight weeks along with brushing at least once a week, and they warn potential owners that Scotties are excellent diggers (this is for both the safety of the dog and the sake of the garden!).

Club members are asked to get in touch with animal shelters and leave their contact information so that they can be reached when needed. Volunteers are on call around the clock for emergencies. About 500 to 600 dogs are rescued each year, most in the range of 3 to 6 years of age, with 75% of them being turned in by the owners for all the "usual" reasons.

Bichons Frises

The US Bichon Frise Rescue Effort has over 30 active rescue representatives who operate in conjunction with the national breed club, the Bichon Frise Club of America, Inc. (www.bichon.org). Would-be adopters are alerted to the fact that Bichons need a great deal of human companionship and interaction, with "-action" being more important than many people think. Bichons look sweet and cuddly, which they are, but this also is an energetic, active breed.

Dogs are surrendered to rescue with the usual complaints regarding expense, care and behavior as are heard throughout purebred rescue. The problem in the case of Bichons is most often due to owners' ignoring that "need of interaction" warning. Bichons are true "people dogs" that need their owners' attention and companionship. The breed also requires extensive grooming and proper bathing in order to maintain

Sweet senior Basset Hound Olive was rescued from a shelter by a Basset rescue group and adopted by a family with another Basset and two Beagles. Olive established herself as "mom" of the pack, and she loves to participate in fun events like "rescue waddles," where she gets to dress up and help raise funds for hounds in need.

that "pure white cloud" look that attracts people to the Bichon in the first place.

Belgian Malinois

An interesting point is made in the American Belgian Malinois Club's (ABMC) rescue format. The breed itself is strongly associated with police and search-dog work; therefore, many Malinois are trained by police departments and search and rescue (SAR) teams. However, Malinois breed rescue states emphatically that they will not place any rescued dog with police officers, trainers or SAR groups. Some Malinois end up in rescue because their trainers felt that the dogs were not up to the exacting job of search and rescue. (Or maybe the dogs just decided they'd rather be perfect pets!)

The ABMC's rescue website (www.malinoisrescue.org) is very well organized, with helpful information for potential adopters as well pictures and full descriptions of the dogs available in different parts of the country. Those hoping to adopt a Malinois must go through the usual in-depth application and interview process, and the rescue highly recommends that potential adopters fill out the "pre-approval" application on their website.

Airedale Terriers

The rescue arm of the Airedale Terrier Club of America (www.airedale.org) is well organized, with regional outlets and an excellent application process.

Mahina was abandoned in poor health and rescued by a German Shepherd rescue group just days before being put to sleep. He is now healthy and happy, volunteering with his new owner as an ambassador for rescue, demonstrating what wonderful dogs are available through adoption.

TOY BREEDS

With the popularity of small dogs here to stay, so is the need for rescue.

Papillons: Papillon Club of America (www.papillonclub.org) Rescue prefers

Yorkie Nikki was adopted into a new family at the age of six after having lived with a family where he was mistreated. Now at age 11, and looking dapper in his raincoat, Nikki is a sweet, loving and healthy boy.

not to ship dogs, so any travel involved in adopting one of their dogs is generally up to the adopter. This may necessitate a hotel stay, since a 24-hour waiting period is also a requirement. The donation asked to adopt a healthy dog up to two years of age runs from $350 to $450. For geriatric or "special needs" dogs, the suggested donation is set on a case-by-case basis. The club warns that Papillons are not great with children since they are too small and fragile for the normal roughhousing of kids. However, they are good with other small dogs as well as with declawed cats. And, of course, they are perfect "people companions."

Yorkshire Terriers: For a small dog, Yorkshire Terrier rescue has a big problem when it comes to rescuing strays. If shelter workers think that a stray dog looks even vaguely like a Yorkie—and it barks—then they figure it must be a Yorkie. Rescue volunteers are called to check out many of these supposed Yorkies that prove to be false alarms.

Yorkshire Terriers, like other toy breeds, are often turned over to rescue because they have not been house-trained. Dogs that are so close to the ground (or the floor) can urinate and even defecate without their owners being aware of it. Not being able to catch the dog in the act makes house-training difficult for an owner who is not alert to the problem.

Another reason is the owner's disregard of the warning that this dog "must be brushed every day." Even a pet coat that is clipped must be brushed. So once again, we have dogs being turned over to rescue through no fault of their own. Learn more about the Yorkshire Terrier Club of America's rescue efforts at www.ytca.org.

Poodles: The Poodle Club of America (PCA) has a national rescue coordinator and also lists contact information on its website (www. poodleclubofamerica.org) for the Poodle clubs around the country and their rescue chairpeople, where applicable. The PCA is the parent club for the three varieties of Poodle, so rescues take in Toy, Standard and Miniature Poodles. To contact Poodle rescue in your area, visit the PCA website, where a clickable map leads you to the club closest to you. The Poodle's best interests are well represented across the US, with multiple clubs found in quite a few states.

Maltese: The American Maltese Association (www.americanmaltese .org) has operated a national rescue program since 1995. In addition to fostering and placing homeless Maltese, they also offer help to Maltese owners who are coping with behavioral issues so that they will be more likely to keep their dogs. The rescue committee consists of a national coordinator and regional coordinators for the East, West and Midwest, with a network of volunteers throughout the country. The first step in the adoption process is filling out the adoption application, which is available online along with other rescue forms.

Chihuahuas: The Chihuahua Club of America (www.chihuahuaclubof america.com) lists contact information for its national coordinator as well as regional contacts and also provides a link to Chihuahua Rescue and Transport (CRT), found at www.chih uahua-rescue.com. This is a nationwide organization "dedicated to rescue, adoption and the medical care of stray and homeless Chihuahuas in need, and to help control the growing overpopulation through spaying and neutering all the dogs in our care."

Some of CRT's policies include spaying/neutering every single dog before adoption and performing mandatory home visits. CRT rescue is broken down into 12 regions, and they only adopt dogs within their given region to facilitate home visits, counseling of adopters and being able to take the dog back into rescue if the placement doesn't work out. The group's adoption process is spelled out in detail on its website, and available dogs are listed by region.

Pomeranians: The American Pomeranian Club (http://american pomeranianclub.org) warns potential adopters not to turn to rescue if they are looking for dogs to breed. They also advise, since Poms often end up in rescue due to house-training problems, that first-time adopters consider an older Pom, who will be easier to train and who will bond just as quickly to his new family. More advice and breed information is followed by a listing of regional club contacts. There are Pom clubs in 31 states, some states having more than one.

FACING PAGE: Bogie, an Airedale rescued in New England.

The number of dogs brought into rescue is not overwhelming due to the fact that the breed is not at the top of the popularity polls. An even bigger reason may be due to the fact that the breed is free of the genetic health problems affecting some of the other large breeds, and thus they live out healthy lives with their original owners.

Approximately 650 Airedales are rescued nationally every year and, again, local placements are given first priority. Mixed breeds that may be part Airedale are not usually taken into the rescue program, although on occasion Airedale rescue volunteers have been known to help out with these dogs.

The group encounters what has become common to all rescuers of large dogs. A common situation is when an elderly person who had an Airedale earlier in life acquires a puppy only to realize a year or two later that the size and strength of the adult dog is more than he can now handle. Management of a large dog is just one reason that a personal visit with adoption applicants by volunteers is an essential part of rescue placement.

As with so many breeds, another leading cause for Airedales to end up in rescue is the proliferation of condominiums (and the scarcity of large-dog-loving landlords). People are

Barnyard pals, Murphy and Buckwheat.

A rescue Welshie and a Miniature Schnauzer friend take part in a "terrier walk."

You can see why an in-depth screening process is so necessary to find the right owners for rescue Airedales.

Welsh Terriers

The Welsh Terrier Club of America Rescue, or WTCARES (www.wtcares.org), rescues approximately 100 dogs per year and has a sizable waiting list. They also help breeders with older dogs to rehome (not sell) by passing along their contact information to applicants on the waiting list who might be a good match for such dogs.

There are six regional Welsh Terrier clubs covering the country under the aegis of the parent club. Regional club members stand by to help adoptive families who encounter minor problems before they become major ones, helping the dogs and their new families to stay together. They've also been known to "rescue" Welsh

changing jobs and moving around more than ever before. Often the dog doesn't fit into the owners' future plans and is considered expendable.

The Airedale is also a breed with a strong personality and needs an owner who understands him. In describing the breed, one Airedale rescue group puts it this way: "If you like a dog you can control completely, you won't like an Airedale."

Terriers whose owners are in sudden need of emergency assistance with such things as short-term care or transportation of their dogs.

Portuguese Water Dogs

The Portuguese Water Dog Club of America's Rescue and Relocation Program (www.pwdca.org) has, in addition to rescuing and rehoming dogs, an objective not

A favorite pastime of these rescue Welsh Terrier housemates is taking each other for walks...here, the 6-year-old is ready to go, but the 14-year-old says, "No, don't make me!"

REGIONAL CLUBS

If everything is a "go," and you and a rescue dog prove to be a match, there will be continued personal involvement with the volunteer, including a follow-up visit during the trial period to answer your questions or help with any problems. Be sure to find out about any regional breed clubs in your area. There's not likely to be one in your hometown but there might be one within a reasonable distance.

Most national breed clubs today have regional offshoots spread out across the country. They operate under the auspices of the parent clubs but serve a given area with a few different capabilities. Their members are breeders, conformation exhibitors, performance-event enthusiasts, stay-at-home pet owners and other breed rescuers. A regional club may put on an AKC-sanctioned match for its breed or host a specialty show sanctioned by the parent club, but for owners of rescue dogs they provide nearby support, friendship and pet-oriented activities.

A regional club's get-togethers may include anything from a lure-coursing event to an introduction to rally obedience to the Canine Good Citizen test. They may hold a picnic for owners and dogs, a health or grooming seminar or just a fun event that offers prizes for the best trick, longest tail, funniest costume or loudest bark. The regional club is "user-friendly" and meant to bring people and dogs together.

specifically brought up by many other groups. This group not only performs all of the normal rescue functions but also helps any PWD owner who is having a

Portuguese Water Dog Chili was close to euthanasia after spending over a month in a shelter, but thankfully he was spotted by a PWD breeder and taken into rescue. His foster family decided to add him to their family pack of PWDs and had him registered with an ILP so he could compete in agility and water trials, in which he's earning titles.

problem with his dog. The group's aim is to prevent the dog from being turned over to rescue in the first place, something other breed rescue groups might want to consider. All club members help with rescue and as mentors to those adopting the dogs. They follow up on rescue placements and pledge to take back any dog whose placement does not work out.

Coonhounds and Foxhounds

These breeds, as well as coonhound and foxhound mixes, face a similar problem as Beagles in that they are often used as hunting dogs and end up in shelters for the same reasons. Hound rescuers work hard, but there are not a large number of hound rescues nationwide, and many hounds and hound mixes are found in shelters. Further, these breeds are not that well known to the general public and can be overlooked for adoption. The truth is that, despite their hunting origins and some people's misconceptions that they are "outdoor dogs," the truth is that hounds make wonderful, affectionate pets that really enjoy attention and the comforts of home.

The Black and Tan Coonhound has a well-organized national rescue effort to help the breed. American Black and Tan Coonhound Rescue, Inc. (www.coonhoundrescue.com) has a national coordinator along with coordinators in various regions of the country and a network of foster homes. This group takes in Black and Tans and mixes, and also has a page with listings of hounds in need from other groups and shelters.

There are a few other "all-hound" rescues spread out around the country. Often these types of hound rescues take in all types of coonhounds, foxhounds and mixes thereof, and some take Beagles and Beagle mixes as well. These rescues also sometimes have referral pages on their websites to list other hounds up for adoption but not in their care.

INDEFINITE LISTING PRIVILEGE— NOT "PAPERS"

People are often annoyed when told they will not be getting the American Kennel Club registration documents (or "papers," as they are often called) for a rescued purebred dog that they are adopting. The breeder is not required to transfer the dog's AKC registration to you in the case of rehoming. Rescue groups also do not pass on the registration papers (in the unlikely event that they should even happen to have them), in part to protect the anonymity of the previous owner.

However, let's say Barney is still of an age to participate in any of the numerous American Kennel Club performance events such as agility, lure coursing, earthdog tests, hunt tests, obedience, rally, etc. He can still enter any of these activities for which he is qualified (some are breed-specific) with what is called an Indefinite Listing Privilege, or ILP.

When you are certain you are going to keep Barney, and when you and he are ready to get involved in these brainy, fun events, you can apply to the American Kennel Club for an ILP. The AKC calls Indefinite Listing Privilege the "program that provides purebred dogs a second chance." This program allows unregistered dogs of breeds recognized by the AKC to compete in AKC events other than conformation showing; many rescued purebreds compete in these events with their ILP numbers.

FROM POUND TO PRECINCT: WHO'S SAFER NOW?

By Diane Jessup

Sitting in Ontario's Gerogina Shelter, the skinny red dog was just one more pit bull slated to die soon. Attorney General Michael Bryant had gotten his wish: Ontario was soon to enact his bill banning American Pit Bull Terriers, American Staffordshire Terriers and Staffordshire Bull Terriers.

Despite the fact that pit bull bites ranked low in the statistics, Michael Bryant had worked long and hard to see that pit bulls would be banned in the province of Ontario. "Mark my words," the attorney general said, "Ontario will be safer." And so the warm-eyed red pit bull, name unknown, had to die for the safety of Ontario's citizenry.

The call went out to pit bull rescue groups across Canada and America: help save Ontario pit bulls facing death or transfer to research facilities. Bullies in Need, an Ontario group formed to save animals impacted by the breed ban, located rescuers in Washington State willing to take two dogs, one of which was the quiet red pit bull in the Gerogina Shelter.

Putting together a transport to move two pit bulls 2,500 miles and across national lines proved very daunting, and the deadline for the dogs was fast approaching. Finally, through the work of several dedicated volunteers, a veterinary clinic that boarded the dogs at no charge for a week and an anonymous benefactor who stepped forward to pay for the flight to Seattle, the pit bulls were loaded onto their freedom flight.

While being transported the dogs were dubbed Nitro and Neville. Nitro began life in America with a new family, and Neville, the skinny red dog, settled in with Carina Collard as a foster dog looking for a new life. Carina's house is a typical rescue house, full of kids, adults, cats, dogs and birds, and Neville fit right in. He was well mannered and peaceful. And my, did he like to play ball with the kids!

As word about Neville got around, suggestions were made to Carina to have the dog tested by Diane Jessup with the LAWDOGS program to see if perhaps he would qualify to be a police detection dog. He seemed to have the ball drive, but what were the chances that this rather mild pit bull would have what it took to become a true working K-9?

When Diane met Neville, she knew instantly that this dog was special. He was polite and sensible, yet possessed an unquenchable desire to hunt for his toy. Excited, she called the Washington State Patrol and advised them that she had a prospect for their upcoming bomb-dog class. WSP trainers met with Diane, Neville was put through his paces and the trainers were pleased.

Neville was accepted by the WSP K-9 program and began training. He had a slow start due to some medical issues, but quickly became a star. When the time came to decide which dogs should proceed to graduation and which should be recycled, Neville came from behind to edge out his Labrador teammate. Neville graduated in August 2005 at a ceremony at the Washington State Capital Campus and began working as a bomb-detection K-9 with his handler, Officer Dixon.

Officer Dixon is the perfect match for Neville: kind, humorous and easygoing. He has taught Neville several tricks, as Neville gets a lot of attention from the public when working. Dixon and Neville examine close to 300 vehicles a day, looking for explosives. They are assigned to a high-risk target, the Washington State ferry system.

Diane Jessup of LAWDOGS laughs when recalling Ontario Attorney General Michael Bryant's words concerning banning pit bulls. "He said, 'Mark my words, Ontario will be safer,' but in reality, he simply kicked out one of the best dogs Ontario had, and now American citizens are safer because Neville is here."

Neglect from his previous owners never succeeded in breaking Bubby's spirit. This dog always gives unconditional love and thankfully found new owners who reciprocate his loving companionship.

With a face that could melt any heart and a personality to match, it's no surprise that Bubby was chosen to do humane education presentations at schools with local animal-control officers. He's a true love of a dog who is always ready to give "Bubby kisses."

EMERGENCY: PIT BULL RESCUE
By Holly Bukes,
President, Pit Bull Rescue Central

Pit Bull rescue is in a state of emergency in the United States. The term "pit bull" is typically used to describe three breeds of dog: the American Pit Bull Terrier, American Staffordshire Terrier and Staffordshire Bull Terrier. These breeds and their mixes are estimated to make up a disproportionate 26% of today's animal shelter populations.

Many shelters have implemented "no-adoption" policies for these breeds, giving in to a media barrage aimed at portraying pit bulls as indiscriminate killers. In the few shelters that do attempt to find homes for select pit bulls, such extreme care must be taken to ensure that these dogs are not adopted for criminal purposes (notably dog fighting) that it is increasingly rare for one of them to find a permanent home of its own.

Shelters often rely upon breed rescue organizations to help these dogs find permanent homes. While only a very small percentage do find adoptive homes, it's important that this grassroots rescue effort exists for these dogs.

As with other types of breed rescue, networking between groups and rescuers is crucial. In this way, more dogs can be helped. It takes an average of six long months to find a good home for a pit bull. In addition, there are areas of the country where overpopulation is worse than

others, and often more opportunities arise for these dogs through networking.

Pit Bull Rescue Central (PBRC) is a unique resource for those doing pit bull rescue, as well as for those hoping to learn more about pit bulls. This Internet-based nonprofit offers free dog listings and marketing services to caretakers of homeless pit bulls and pit bull mixes. Dogs must be spayed or neutered prior to being posted on the website. PBRC's website, www. pbrc.net, has become the "go to" website for those looking to adopt a pit bull or pit bull mix.

Pit Bull Rescue Central also offers a preliminary online adoption application available for completion by potential adopters. PBRC volunteers provide a pre-screening of all applications received, which are forwarded to the dog's caretakers. A wealth of educational material is available on the site for use by anyone who would like to know more about pit bulls, including their typical temperament and behavior. PBRC is committed to educating current and potential pit bull owners alike so that they have a better understanding of their dogs' unique nature and heritage. This leads to responsible and caring ownership. As pit bulls are not the dogs for everyone, it's critical that rescuers and adopters understand their special nature and background in order to make suitable placements.

TOP: Tonka with Timmy, one of the nine cats with whom he shares his home in addition to a female rescued pit bull. **BOTTOM:** Tonka's owner describes him as a "75-pound goofball," and his adorable smile seems to say it all. Tonka was given up by his original owner when he moved to an area with breed-specific legislation prohibiting pit bulls, but when his new owner met Tonka there was no question that he was going home with her!

Stray dog Lily was covered in ticks and was heartworm positive when she was picked up. This beautiful and now-healthy pit bull was adopted by a loving family in Virginia.

Picked up as a stray, Pandora was healthy but scared and unsocialized. She now enjoys life with her forever family and her "brother," a neutered male pit bull who is her best friend.

Dumped and left for dead, Precious thankfully was found and brought to a rescuer who helped her overcome her physical and mental trauma. She now happily gets along with dogs and cats, loves going for car rides and does her "happy dance" every day at dinnertime. She is a true inspiration and touches the hearts of all who meet her.

These pups were born to a female pit bull who was owned by an animal collector; she had over 25 unaltered pit bulls and eventually surrendered them to rescue. These pups were spayed/neutered and adopted to new homes through rescue programs.

Pit bulls are wonderful, fun-loving dogs who have become some of the most abused and neglected dogs in our society. Because there are so many who need homes, and so few who will find them, dogs that are true breed ambassadors should be selected for placement. These breed ambassadors will then go on to make a positive impression and educate others, making the world a better place for these often misunderstood canines. Pit bulls have certainly been known to wiggle their way into the hearts of unsuspecting animal advocates and dog lovers!

Titan escaped euthanasia at a shelter because the animal-control officer took a special liking to him. He was adopted by a police officer and is a true ambassador for the breed, as his owner has encouraged others to adopt rescued pit bulls.

GREYHOUND ADOPTION: AN INTERNATIONAL COMMUNITY

By Cindy Victor, Northern Lights Greyhound Adoption

My entry into the world of Greyhound adoption began when I looked through a window at the University of Minnesota Small Animal Hospital and saw six tall and lean dogs standing shoulder to shoulder, watching me watch them. Greyhounds, I thought, even though I didn't know this breed. I was at the hospital because my male German Shepherd Dog was very ill. My female GSD was old and frail. Looking at the beauty and peacefulness of the six Greyhound blood donors, I knew I was seeing my future.

There have always been retired racing Greyhounds living as pets, but Greyhound adoption really took off in the 1980s. Today there are hundreds of Greyhound rescue groups throughout the US, Canada, Europe and Australia. The Greyhound Project (www.adopt-a-greyhound.org) is a source for finding a group in your area as well as specialized services such as the Golden Years Senior Greyhound Referral Programs.

Greyhound Pets of America, founded in 1987, has adopted over 65,000 Greyhounds into loving homes and today has 52 chapters, according to GPA's national president, Rory Goree. GPA is host to the web radio program

Adoption events and get-togethers are popular with Greyhound rescuers, who enjoy the opportunity to introduce new people to the breed, have adopters meet the available dogs and let owners and dogs socialize.

Volunteers and adoptable Greyhounds at an adoption event held by Grateful Greyhounds, a New York-based rescue group.

"Greyhounds Make Great Pets," covering topics as diverse as raising racing puppies, selecting a pet sitter and coping with the loss of a pet.

The National Greyhound Association, a non-profit association that is offi-cially recognized by the Greyhound racing industry as the sole registry for racing Greyhounds on the North American continent, has joined hands with organized Greyhound adoption to ensure placement of retired racers into homes. Gary Guccione, executive director of NGA, estimates that 20,000 retired racers are being adopted in America each year. Currently every US track has its own adoption program or is affiliated with one or more rescues in the area.

Why do we adopt retired racers? It's not out of necessity or pity. Nittany Greyhounds in Pennsylvania suggests these reasons: Greyhounds are affec-tionate, well-behaved, intelligent and easy to train. They shed minimally and have little or no odor. Most don't bark. They're terrific travelers. Most retire between 2 and 4 years of age, and they have a life expectancy of 12 to 14 years. Fifty percent of them can live compatibly with cats. Some people allergic to dogs aren't allergic to Greyhounds, due to the breed's short, sleek coat and skin type. You don't have to bend over to pet them.

I would add that Greyhounds are irresistibly beautiful and amusing and that adopting a Greyhound brings friends to your life. We are a community of like-minded, supportive people who are gaga over these gentle couch potatoes who strike dramatic poses in sleep. We take our dogs to "meet and greets" at pet stores, wineries and fairs. Our adoption groups hold picnics

Potential adopters, owners and rescuers alike enjoy a fun day out dedicated to helping this wonderful breed.

where all are welcome. Want to see 200 beautiful dogs in 16 color combinations, all getting along with each other and not barking? Go to a Greyhound picnic. Want to see thousands of Greyhounds getting along and not barking? Make the annual "Greyhounds Reach the Beach" reunion in Dewey Beach, Delaware your October destination.

Many of us get involved. Foster homes for newly retired racers are always needed. People volunteer for the Greyhound Underground Railroad, transporting dogs to distant homes. Some fly Galgos, the Greyhounds of Spain, to America. Essential to the cause are volunteers who haul dogs from the track to the adoption group.

Nittany Greyhounds' Jo Langer loves the four-hour drive to a kennel in Connecticut to pick up dogs. She always sits in the back of the van to ensure that none gets out of hand. "There's huge satisfaction in helping them transition from their racing lives to their retirement lives," said Langer, who sometimes brings one of the dogs home to foster. "The best part is when the dog, cleaned and fed, settles into warm puffy blankets and falls asleep with a contented sigh."

Getting a retired racer ready for adoption doesn't happen overnight. Northern Lights Greyhound Adoption in Minnesota is based in an animal hospital. Its website, www.nlgamn.org, has pictures of what happens between a dog's arrival from the track and becoming available for adoption. The steps include bathing; intestinal parasite exam and control; flea and tick control; collection of blood samples for heartworm, Lyme and *Ehrlichia canis* testing; a physical exam; surgical prep for spaying or neutering; nail trimming; dental prophylaxis; daily toothbrushing; and weekly application of a plaque preventive. Not least, Ali, NLGA's fearless kitty, determines whether the dog is cat-safe.

All groups have their adopters sign an adoption agreement. To adopt from Greyhound Adoption of Greater Rochester, New York, one must agree to always keep the dog on leash when outdoors, except in a completely enclosed area; have the dog wear GAGR's ID tag on a Greyhound-safe (martingale) collar; immediately notify GAGR and animal control should the dog become lost or stolen; return the dog to GAGR if for any reason custody must be relinquished; and not give the dog away to any person without express permission from the group. GAGR adopters also pledge not to leave the dog outside unattended under any circumstances, keep the dog crated when he is home alone until he is acclimated and can safely be left uncrated, allow the dog to relieve himself at least four times a day, never tie out or chain the dog and, throughout the dog's life, use heartworm preventive, ensure dental hygiene and maintain vaccinations as required by law.

Does this sound like a lot to expect from adopters? Every Greyhound owner I know would be able to think of something missing from the list. In my opinion, adopters should pledge to give daily tummy rubs!

Thanks to Greyhound rescue, many retired racers are now loved and loving family members.

BRANDY'S STORY

By Andrea and Patrick Kelly, American Bullmastiff Association Rescue

ABOVE: Brandy, post-surgery. **BELOW:** Brandy's amazing recovery led to one milestone after another.

One bright summer day I got a call about an elderly Bullmastiff in a New York City shelter. She was blind and mostly deaf, barely able to walk, but she bravely greeted everyone with a wagging tail. Her nose worked fine as she sniffed out a friendly hand, coming to rest her body against my legs, instantly winning my heart.

When Brandy stepped into the sunshine, I examined her closely. Her eyes were crusted shut and she had severe entropion. Her ears dripped with black ooze and she appeared to be toothless. Her feet were infected and she limped badly in front. She choked and coughed constantly.

My husband Patrick came home and met the new "foster child." To my relief, he said she needed a ramp for the van and an elevated food dish, and he got right to work. Later, he took her for her evening stroll. From that moment, Brandy became his dog.

Surgery was inevitable: we opted to correct the entropion and remove some wrinkles from her muzzle to ease her breathing. The cysts came off and her swollen gums were cut back to reveal her teeth. Sutures ran from the edge of her lip, up over her muzzle, all the way down the other side and around both eyes.

As she began to heal, we noticed an amazing thing—she could see out of the bottoms of her eyes! The wrinkles on her muzzle had pressed her lower lids up over her corneas, protecting them from the inward-turning eyelashes. Everything on the farm was new for this city girl, but her favorite sight was her dad's truck pulling into the driveway.

Brandy improved every day, and she began to accompany us to agility lessons. At first she watched, but when she was stronger she joined in. Agility nationals approached, and Brandy set off with us, making new friends wherever she went. Upon returning, we began serious training. In true Brandy fashion, she passed the TDI (Therapy Dogs International) test not quite three months after leaving the shelter.

Next she ran in her first agility trial, flawlessly completing two NADAC (North American Dog Agility Council) tunnelers' courses. Later that month, Brandy went to the American Bullmastiff Association national specialty in Wisconsin and showed in Novice obedience, charming the crowd with her enthusiasm and courage. She led the rescue parade and took first prize in the costume event dressed as Cleopatra, with her dad as Marc Antony.

The following spring, Brandy earned her first leg toward a rally obedience title; in October, she entered a second trial and got two more qualifying scores for the Association of Pet Dog Trainers' title of R1 (Rally-O Level 1).

ABOVE: Brandy enjoyed attending events where she could be an ambassador for rescue (and she didn't mind the ice cream, either!). **BELOW:** A true "daddy's girl."

That summer, Brandy attended the Mayor's Alliance event in Central Park, showing spectators all of the advantages of adopting an older dog. She attended the following year too, in her "chariot," and spent the afternoon charming the public, eating ice cream and comforting a frightened one-eyed Maltese.

Although Brandy was only with us for a few years, the strength of her spirit will always live on with us. All she overcame, all she accomplished and the unconditional love she gave inspire us in our rescue efforts every day.

One big happy family! Shepherd-mix
pup Dixie **(LEFT)** was adopted from an
all-dog rescue group, and Jeager
(RIGHT) was adopted from the
family's veterinarian.

CHAPTER 5

Adopting from a Rescue Group

THE RESCUE DOG COMES FIRST

All types of good rescue groups, purebred and all-dog alike, follow a similar basic adoption procedure. The details vary from group to group, but here we will discuss an overview of the typical adoption process. Of course, one thing that every reputable rescue holds dear is that the welfare of the dog always comes first. The wishes of the prospective adopter follow a close second. A perfect match is the aim of every rescue group and volunteer, so they need to know as much as they possibly can about both the dogs and the would-be adopters. For example, if a potential adoptive family has a lifestyle where no one is home all day, they may have a longer wait until a dog who is accustomed to that type of routine is available. Not every dog can go all day without a potty break or sit home alone with nothing to do.

When a dog comes into rescue for whatever reason, the rescue volunteer taking in the dog gets as much information about him as possible. The dog is then officially signed over to the rescue group, whether by the owners who are surrendering him or the shelter or animal-control officer who is turning him over. Caring for the dog begins with a complete physical exam by a veterinarian. Immunizations are updated and an overall health assessment is

When adopting a dog, the ages and lifestyles of all family members must be considered to find the right match. Baby likes nothing more than snuggling up for some "girl talk."

SETTLING IN

For many rescued dogs in new homes, there can be a lengthy period of adjustment before they can be left alone without becoming panic-stricken. Separation anxiety runs high in dogs that are unsure of their new lives. It may take time before a rescued dog is comfortable with his new routine, new "family pack" and new living quarters.

done. Any health problems that are discovered are evaluated and treated. If this is the best time for it, the dog may be neutered or spayed (if he or she is not already). The dog also is thoroughly cleaned up and groomed.

Next, the dog's source of rescue or previous home is considered. In the case of an owner-surrendered dog, the reason for the dog's being turned over, or as much as is known about it, is considered as well. The dog then goes to a suitable foster home. Most

CONSIDER THE KIDS

Responsible breeders as well as most rescue organizations are cautious about placing dogs (especially puppies) in families with very young children. Six to ten years of age is usually perfect. Toddlers cannot be expected to differentiate between a soft warm puppy and a stuffed toy. The toy can be tossed, dragged around or shoved in a toy box. A puppy treated that way can be hurt and/or will defend himself—with teeth. Around the age of four or five, children can become little dictators. Mom and Dad are the head honchos and, therefore, in the child's eyes, the dog is a lower-class citizen to be ordered about. The dog, on the other hand, looks at a young child as his littermate, and he'll take just so much bossing around before he stands up for himself. Dogs have no hands, so they use their mouths, and puppies have very, very sharp teeth!

Children under the age of about ten should not be given too much responsibility for the care of a dog, in spite of the fact that they keep telling you they can do it all, and even promise that they will. They mean well, and are sincere in their desire at that very moment, but they are kids! Caring for the dog soon begins to interfere with their other activities. If you, the parents, aren't up to assuming full responsibility when all of those promises fly out the window, you will be frustrated and the puppy will be the one to suffer.

Older kids are a perfect match for a dog. Dogs don't tell secrets. Dogs don't make fun of you or criticize you. Dogs forgive you no matter what you've done wrong. Dogs are true, trustworthy pals. For an only child, a dog can be a very special, very best pal. Owning a dog gives any child the opportunity to develop into a more caring, thoughtful, unselfish person—all of the good things that are very hard to teach with just words.

rescue groups do not have physical facilities for housing dogs; rather, the rescued dogs live in volunteers' homes while awaiting placement. In the foster homes, the volunteers do intensive assessments of the dogs' personalities, temperaments, likes and dislikes, general behavior, social skills, house-training— all of the elements needed to determine what type of home and family will be best for each particular dog. Volunteers also keep up with their foster dogs' grooming and any healthcare needs.

Fostering rescue dogs is where volunteers are due high praise. It's a lot of work, often very difficult physically and emotionally. The only payback is the satisfaction of knowing that the dog is being given another chance for a good life, but this is more than enough reward for dedicated foster parents.

THE ADOPTION PROCEDURE

After a prospective adopter makes initial contact with the rescue group and expresses interest in adopting a rescued dog, he must fill out a long, detailed application. (No cheating—every answer gets checked!) Each rescue group operates somewhat differently, depending on the size of their operation, the number of dogs they deal with and the number of "super-people" (a.k.a. volunteers) they have available. What follows is a generalization of the adoption procedure.

First, your application must be approved by the rescue in order to continue. Following approval of your application, several things can happen. If you've expressed interest in a

Penny, formerly Showcase Leila, has really blossomed since retiring from Greyhound racing.

particular dog that the group has available, you will be told whether or not that dog will be suitable for you and your lifestyle. If not, the rescue volunteers may suggest one or more dogs that could be suitable for you. In a different scenario, you may be told that there are no dogs currently available or that none of the available dogs are the right match for you. In either of the latter cases, as long as your application is approved the rescue will keep you on a waiting list for just the right dog.

Then there is that all-important home visit in which a rescue volunteer will come to your home. He may bring the dog that you're interested in, may not bring a dog at all or, if you're dealing with a purebred rescue, may not bring the dog that is available for adoption but one of the same breed to see how you get along with the breed on your own turf. Applicants often do not realize, for example, just how big a big dog actually is or just how active a small dog can

be until they see the dog in their own home. By meeting a dog of the breed, you get to see for yourself, and there's time to change your mind.

After the usual pleasantries, the volunteer will dive into specific questions such as:

- "I don't see the 4-foot fencing you said you had. Can you show me?"

SO YOU WANT TO ADOPT A DOG...

And you know that there are many homeless dogs in need. How do you find out where all of these dogs are available? The Internet is a great place to start. If you have a specific breed in mind, you can usually find links to local or regional rescue contacts through the national breed club's website. You can search sites like Pet finder.com for dogs of a certain breed or for shelters and rescues in your area who will have a variety of dogs for you to meet. Another great place to look is at your local vet's office. Many have bulletin boards with postings from local adoption groups that tell of their upcoming events. Owners looking for new homes for their dogs often post flyers in vets' offices as well. Also, many pet-supply stores allow animal-adoption groups to hold "meet and greets" in their stores, where you can find out about (and often meet!) available animals.

Rescue volunteers evaluate the dogs to find out if they will be suitable for homes with small children. Lab mix Baci (**LEFT**) and shepherd mix Rocco (**RIGHT**) happily fit the bill, and they are loving companions to their two "sisters."

- "What kind of cover do you have for that lovely pool?"
- "You mentioned that your grandchildren visit. Do those cute little kids next door also come over?"
- "I know you want a dog for companionship, but how about exercise such as daily walks, rain or shine? Are you up to it?"
- "Are you familiar with the grooming required by this breed?"

And so on.

This will be a completely friendly visit and is not meant to be intimidating, but the volunteer has to get as much nitty-gritty information as possible to first make sure that you can provide a suitable home for a dog and then to put you and the "right" dog together. Many of the questions you'll be asked will be similar to those asked on the adoption application, but the volunteer will want to verify your answers and get into more detail. All of this is purely in the best interest of the dog, as one change of homes is enough for any dog.

- "I noticed two pretty cats on the porch. They aren't mentioned on the application; are they yours?"
- "May I see where the dog will be left when you go out?"
- "How many hours did you say there'd be no one home?"

The volunteer will also want to chat about any previous dog(s) you've owned. If dealing with a purebred rescue, the volunteer will ask about your familiarity (or lack of it) with this specific breed and will discuss its good points ("This breed makes an excellent family dog and loves kids") and the not-so-good ones ("They'll dig up your whole back yard and wonder why you're not pleased with the result"). With any dog, purebred or mixed, the volunteer will discuss the need for obedience training, perhaps going so far as to suggest a local trainer or classes; things like the amount and type of routine exercise; feeding tips;

ADOPTION: A FAMILY DECISION

When the parents decide that the family is ready for a canine addition, and the kids are old enough to accept their roles as partial caretakers of a dog, then it is definitely the right moment to sit down for a family conference. There will be much to discuss. For starters, discuss the kinds of dog that might be suitable until everyone can agree on what you are looking for. If a few different pure breeds appeal to you, visiting an all-breed dog show where you can see the different dogs and even talk to breeders and handlers is a good idea. If the kids want a Collie, but that's too big a dog for your home, have a look at Shetland Sheepdogs. By meeting people in the various breeds, you can express interest in a rescue dog and find out whom to contact in your area. If you'd like an all-American mutt, visit some local shelters or check out the websites of local all-dog rescue groups to see what dogs are available. Each mixed-breed dog is an individual, so you will want to meet the dogs that interest you and see if your personalities mesh.

When you've narrowed it down to what type of dog is right for your family, there are other things to consider. Should it be a puppy or an older dog? (The pros and cons of that are numerous.) Who will be responsible for grooming? How will the dog fit into the family's everyday routine? What about house-training? Who will take the dog to obedience classes? How much exercise will the dog need, and how, when and where will he get his exercise? What will it cost to maintain the dog?

By having open discussions and making it a family decision, everyone in the household will feel that they've had a part in selecting the dog. It's also an excellent way to begin teaching children the reality of responsible dog ownership. It's not all just playing catch in the back yard!

FIND YOUR MATCH ON PETFINDER

In the vast world of the Internet, Petfinder (www.petfinder.com) has become a well-known place online that brings together shelters, rescue groups, the dogs they help and the people who want to adopt them. Many shelters and rescues across the country have signed on to Petfinder, where they can set up individual sites with information about them, their policies and the animals they have available for adoption. The result is a wealth of information for potential adopters, who can search Petfinder for pets to adopt by location (US and Canada), type of animal, breed/mix, age, sex and other parameters. Petfinder updates its site regularly with helpful and timely topics to help potential adopters. Current and future pet owners alike will enjoy the resource library, which contains articles on a wide range of topics from the practical to the heartwarming. A calendar section allows shelters and rescues to post upcoming events, and there is even a special section just for animal-loving kids. You can even shop for products for both people and animals through Petfinder's partner site, the Animal Rescue Site (www.the animalrescuesite.com). Proceeds go toward feeding homeless animals.

If you like to interact with other adoption-minded individuals, you can visit the message boards to discuss rescue topics, post or read alerts about dogs in need (including urgent cases) and arrange or volunteer for transports. Users can also chat about many general pet-related topics such as animal care, lost and found pets, stories about their own pets, jobs in the pet field and more.

Anyone can log on to Petfinder to use the pet search and access many of the site's features. However, there are some special options available only to those who register on the site, such as being able to save recent pet searches. Those who have an adoption success story can sign up to submit their "Happy Tails" to share with other animal lovers and potential new owners.

basic grooming; and any health issues, including the possible cost of subsequent medical care should a problem arise. Breed rescuers will discuss breed-specific healthcare, characteristics and "fun stuff" about the breed. If you are interested in and are meeting a specific dog, the volunteer will tell you about the particular dog and what the rescue has learned about him since he's been in their care.

If all goes well, you'll be told what the chances are of your getting this (or another) dog, and approximately when that might happen. If you have your eye on a specific dog, and all members of the family have met him and love him (and vice versa), you may have a new addition to your home fairly soon. If the rescue volunteer doesn't feel that you and this dog are a good match, or if you've changed your mind about the dog after meeting him in person, the rescuer will let you know when his group has a good potential match for you to meet. Again, some rescues have many dogs waiting for good homes; with others, you must be prepared to wait. This is especially true with some pure breeds. Remember, working with a rescue group is not like going to a supermarket where you can pick a dog off the shelf like a box of your favorite cereal!

If no particular dog is a match for you at this point, you may find yourself going back to square one and repeating your preferences for age, sex, size or color and how firmly you stand on each of these preferences. If

working with an all- or mixed-breed rescue, you will likely have preferences for a certain breed or combination of breeds. It's fine to have preferences, so long as you understand all, or most, of what's involved in acquiring this type of dog, you feel that you can cope with it and you are not going to change your mind.

On the other hand, the volunteer may now be able to point out why a dog of a particular breed might not be

After an exhausting day of sniffing and standing guard at the front window, it's naptime for Brisco.

suitable for you, your family or your lifestyle, or why it might not be the right time for you to own a dog. Perhaps you are not home enough to take care of a dog, perhaps you should wait until your children are older or perhaps you need to first fence in your yard. With purebred rescue, there may be reasons why a dog of this breed would not be suitable for you, your family or your lifestyle. It works both ways, because after the home visit

THE ADOPTION APPLICATION

While adoption applications vary from rescue to rescue, here is an overview of some things you can expect to see on a typical application:

- Why do you want to adopt a dog?
- What kind of pets, if any, have you owned previously?
- Which of these pets do you still own?
- Which of these pets do you no longer own and what happened to it/them?
- What pets do you currently own (type/age/sex)?
- Are your pets spayed/neutered?
- Who is your current veterinarian and may we contact the vet for a reference? If this is your first pet, what veterinarian do you plan to use?
- Do you own or rent your residence?
- If rent, are pets allowed? Please also provide the name and phone number of your landlord.
- How many people reside in your home and what are their ages?
- Who will have primary responsibility for the dog's feeding, bathroom trips, exercise?
- Will the dog be kept indoors, outdoors or a combination of both? If a combination, how many hours indoors and how many hours outdoors?
- What is the typical weekday schedule for the family members?
- Will the dog be left alone each day and, if so, for how many hours?
- Where will the dog be kept when no one is home?
- Do you have a fenced yard?
- If so, what type and how high?

Again, these are basic questions. Most applications are quite involved, and questions will reflect the adoption policies of the individual rescue groups. Answering all questions honestly and in as much detail as possible only increases your chances of finding a canine companion who will be a great fit for you and your family.

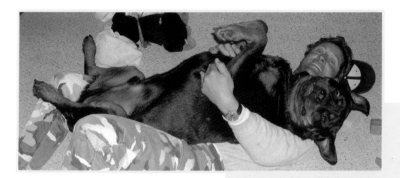

The hope for every rescue is that the dog will be a perfect fit for the family, giving and receiving unconditional love.

you may also decide that this breed is not really what you had in mind or that you're not really ready to own any dog right now. It's better to be sure than sorry. Let the contact person know immediately if you do have a change of heart. The next person waiting in the wings will be pleased to hear that they are indeed next!

MAKING IT OFFICIAL

Once the rescue group has matched you up with the perfect canine companion, it's time to finalize the adoption. Many rescue groups set forth a trial period that includes a follow-up visit with a rescue volunteer to answer your questions, help with any problems and just make sure that all is going well. The rescue will also often stipulate that if things do not work out and the dog is given back to the rescue group before the end of the trial period, your adoption donation will be returned. All of these details will be stated in the adoption agreement, which all reputable rescue groups require adopters to sign.

One of the most important stipulations of the agreement states that, if the placement doesn't work out, you will return the dog to

While some transports move many dogs at a time, others are for a small group or only one dog. A rescuer comforts this Great Dane on a leg of her journey to a Dane rescue, which spanned several states.

RESCUE ON THE ROAD

Dogs in some shelters and rescues today are not necessarily local dogs. That used to be the case, but today dogs are also transported from areas where the adoption rates are low or where there is a surplus of homeless dogs. Since municipal shelters usually serve certain towns or counties and are not allowed to take in dogs from outside their specified areas, transported dogs are most often seen in privately run shelters and rescues. When they have the space, organizations with good adoption rates are often happy to help when they can by taking in dogs from rescues in other parts of the country or from high-kill facilities in areas where they have little chance of being adopted before their time is up. Other times, dogs may be transported from their foster homes to their forever homes.

How are transports that cross multiple states organized? With purebred rescue, rescue groups usually have transport volunteers across the country who can organize a route and split up the driving to move dogs from point A to point B in a relay system. For shelter dogs that are taken in by all-dog or mixed-breed rescues a distance away, there are groups and volunteers dedicated solely to coordinating rescue transports. Some rescue groups have good relationships with shelters in other states and take in dogs regularly, so when the time comes to transport dogs there is usually a set team of volunteers who spring into action. Some people operate transports in which they agree to drive the entire distance, often hundreds of miles, in return for a set donation for each dog. However it happens, a transport requires organization and cooperation between all parties involved.

Since many rescue transports cover long distances, routes are broken up into "legs" so that each driver has a commitment of only a few hours. A driver will pick up the canine passengers at a given location and drive to a meet-up point that may be an hour or two away, where the next driver picks up the dogs, and so on until they reach their destination. The meet-up points are usually places where the drivers can give the dogs a potty break, a short walk and a drink of water before getting on the road again.

The transport coordinator is the person in charge of a transport. This person decides on the date of transport (transports often take place over weekends), figures out the route, makes sure that a driver is assigned to each leg, indicates any special requirements (e.g., dogs on medication, dogs that must be crated while traveling) and collects contact information (phone numbers, makes and models of cars, etc.) for each driver so that everyone can keep in touch during the transport. This person is also the liaison between the sending and the receiving rescue(s)/shelter(s). Depending on the length of the transport, sometimes an overnight stay is required, and the transport coordinator will find someone along the route who is willing to host the canine passengers in his home overnight. Supplies like collars and leashes sometimes travel with the dogs, but the most important things are health documentation and rabies tags. Dogs must have their vaccinations and the necessary health paperwork to cross state lines. In the case of dogs from high-kill shelters that are saved at the last minute, shelter workers and volunteers must be ready to make sure that the dogs are vetted before leaving on the transport.

The Internet is an invaluable tool for helping transports come together. Transport coordinators often build up extensive networks of contacts and send out e-mail pleas for drivers when organizing transports. There are also some e-mail groups solely for posting transport run sheets; some are regional and some are nationwide. These are good ways to reach out to many volunteers across a wide area to fill runs and to make new contacts for future transports.

that group. The all-encompassing statement that the dog is to be returned to the rescue group holds true indefinitely, no matter how far beyond the trial period. It's for the life of the dog. Remember this and honor it;

you are agreeing to it by signing the adoption agreement. If things don't work out down the road, admitting defeat may be hard for you, or your pride, but the dog's welfare is at stake, and that is the bottom line in breed rescue.

THE COST OF RESCUE

How do volunteer rescue organizations pay for all of the work involved and the care given their dogs? Carefully! The work and most of the care is performed by volunteers, but there are many things that a rescue needs money for: veterinary bills, food, accessories, possibly transportation and more.

Part of a rescue's money comes from fees paid by adopters. First there is the application fee, which is generally non-refundable. Beyond that, every rescue group asks for a donation for the adoption of a dog. Usually adoption fees are on a sliding scale depending on the age (or occasionally the health) of the dog. Puppies are on the high end of the scale, since

Rescued from a shelter with a fractured and badly infected back leg, Charley ended up losing his leg despite the rescuer's best efforts to save it. The family who had planned to adopt Charley loved him just the same, four legs or three, and they picked him up a few days after his amputation. The unconditional love with which this family welcomed Charley into their hearts is what rescue is all about.

they are hard to come by and the adopting family gets to enjoy the dog for his entire lifetime. Senior canine citizens and special-needs dogs are more difficult to place, and thus their adoption fee is less. The adoption fee for a dog can range widely, typically anywhere from $100 to up to as much as $500. The cost of mandatory spaying or neutering (if the dog is not yet spayed or neutered) is either included in the donation or is a separate fee; you'll be told which.

Buster models a "Pure Mutt" bandana. Pure Mutt, Inc. sells apparel for dogs and those who love them. The company donates part of its profits to a Florida pet rescue and strives to promote mixed-breed dogs and shelter adoption.

A major portion of a rescue's funding comes from donations, as adoption fees only cover the basic expenses. Adopters may choose to make a donation in excess of the adoption fee, and that is always most gratefully received. Owners also often make donations to rescue groups in memory of their dogs who have passed away. Many rescue groups have options on their websites where people can contribute money with a few simple clicks. Donations are further solicited at rescue-group events and by rescue volunteers on an ongoing basis.

Apart from donations, additional money is raised through fundraising. Some purebred rescue groups hold boutique sales at breed specialty shows or other

A shelter employee with two tuxedoed companions.

Actress Tamara Tunie with Spraga.

Film critic and radio personality Frank DeCaro **(RIGHT)** with partner Jim Colluci **(LEFT)** and their dog Herman.

Steven Schirripa of *The Sopranos*.

Actress and animal rescuer Hallie Kate Eisenberg.

Actress and comedienne Nora Dunn, the evening's master of ceremonies.

Comedienne Reno with Edith Ann.

events, and some breed rescues sell breed-related items on their websites. Rescue groups hold all kinds of events like bake sales, garage sales, raffles and auctions to bring in additional revenue. Some groups hold fun get-togethers like "dog walks" and "dog washes." Some sell merchandise like T-shirts or fun accessories for dogs. Many rescue groups are very creative in the ways that they raise funds, encouraging dogs, owners and the community at large to participate. All monies raised from fundraising go directly to support the rescue program.

So where does all of the money that a rescue group raises go? To start with, there is never enough. Any rescue group will tell you that the minute they think they are in the clear, along comes another emergency. As any pet owner knows, vet bills can add up quickly. Multiply

It's all smiles at Broadway Barks, a fundraiser/adoption event held annually in New York City to raise awareness about homeless pets and to educate the public about responsible pet ownership.

A fan of Mary Tyler Moore, who co-founded Broadway Barks along with Bernadette Peters.

that by the number of dogs in a given rescue group, and costs can be staggering. Money acquired through adoption fees, outside donations and fundraising goes toward such things as veterinary bills, medication, transportation, food, equipment (crates, collars, leashes, bedding, etc.) and, of course, dog toys.

When many dogs are taken in by one group or, in the case of regional purebred rescue, in one region, the expense for care escalates proportionately. One major obstacle is a lack of foster homes in any given area. If a rescue takes in more dogs than they can accommodate, which often happens in order to save lives, dogs must then be housed in breeders' kennels or in commercial boarding kennels until a foster home becomes available. Unfortunately, the breeders and facilities cannot always afford to offer this assistance free of charge, and thus the rescue becomes responsible for boarding fees.

The dogs enjoy the attention and may even meet their new best friends.

NYC-area shelters and rescues get a chance to showcase their many adoptable pets.

Auction items, like these mugs autographed by Broadway stars, raise money to help homeless animals.

Held in the heart of the theater district and produced by Broadway Cares/Equity Fights AIDS, this event brings out animal lovers and theater enthusiasts alike.

The canines are the star performers of the day.

Django had a successful young show
career but his breeder felt that his
affectionate temperament was more
suited to life as a family dog, so she
adopted him out to a new owner who
had carefully researched the breed and
who proved to be a perfect match.

CHAPTER 6

All Roads Lead to Home

Adopting a dog takes place in numerous ways. We've briefly mentioned the term "rehoming." While rehoming is different from rescuing a dog, you are still doing a good thing for a dog that needs a new home for whatever reason.

FROM THE BREEDER

Breeders will occasionally have dogs to place, not just puppies to sell. The easiest type of adoption is when you obtain a dog directly from the breeder from whom you have bought a previous dog. A certain amount of friendship is involved. You know the people you're dealing with, they know you and you know the breed. This is a real no-brainer and the best of all possible worlds.

On the other hand, maybe you had a dog of a certain breed when you were a kid or when your kids were kids, or you've done enough homework to decide that a particular breed is right for you, your family and your lifestyle. You may be familiar with the breed's adult size, coat type and care requirements and even with personality characteristics, temperament and exercise needs. Further, and importantly, each and every member of the family agrees on this breed. After all of these considerations, you decide to contact a breeder to see if he has a dog in need of a new home (maybe a dog that's retired from the show ring). You may luck out; if not, you will perhaps be referred to another breeder or to the breed's rescue group.

Only deal with a reputable breeder who is a member of his national parent breed club. If the breeder has a dog available, he will be upfront about why the dog is available, the dog's health and the dog's temperament, and will take the dog back if the placement doesn't work out. You'll be asked a zillion questions, because a caring breeder only wants the right home for each and every one of his dogs. Bear with it, because both you and the dog benefit from what may seem like an inquisition.

The dog may be a champion, but having a title won't make him any better or worse when it comes to adjusting his lifestyle to that of being your pet. His champion title just means he's handsome, which, of course, all dogs know they are. He's special because the breeder decided it was better for him to live as a pet in a regular home than to live out his years in a kennel. His breeder cares enough about his future to let him go,

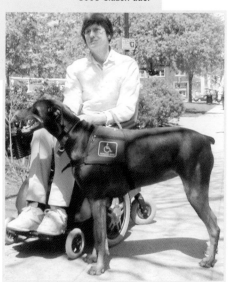

Rescued Doberman U-CD Dare's Terra Firma CD, CGC, TDI is a licensed service dog in addition to holding obedience titles, therapy dog certification and the Canine Good Citizen title.

and you care enough to take him in. You could say that makes him doubly special.

Every now and then, good reputable breeders, even those with small kennels, must cut back on the number of dogs they keep. There are several reasons, other than having retired from showing, why a dog may be available for rehoming. Perhaps a young dog was kept for the conformation show ring and/or future breeding but he hasn't matured as expected. This has nothing to do with the dog's "pet-ability"; rather, he most likely has what is considered by the breed standard to be a "fault" or "undesirable" feature. For example, his tail or ears are not held correctly, he never reached the preferred height (or is above the ideal height), his adult coat didn't come in with the desired color or he has a couple of teeth missing. These things are basic concerns of a good breeder, but none of them interferes at all with the dog's potential as a pet.

BREEDER HELP

If any adoption scenario results in your taking in a purebred dog, you can ask the breeder (if known) or the dog's vet for advice. You can also contact the nearest breed club for the name of someone who can help you with any problems you are having in understanding the dog. Many behaviors are breed-specific and can be easily explained. Even if you're not having any problems, you may just need some advice on grooming or healthcare. You may need someone to recommend a good vet and/or boarding kennel in your area if you don't live near the dog's original home. Breeders and breed-club members, via their hobby, have a network that covers the entire country. If you should be unlucky enough to reach an unresponsive person, don't give up. The next one you contact is bound to be more helpful. And, in the event you cannot keep the dog, you'll have made a good connection for breed rescue.

A breeder may keep a dog for a couple of years to see whether the fault corrects itself. If it doesn't, rather than let the dog live out his life in the kennel, the breeder finds him a good home. Rehoming can also occur when an older dog has not produced in his or her pups the qualities that the breeder is seeking. Another situation is when the dog has reached the age when his or her career as stud dog or brood bitch is over. These ages vary according to the particular breed's longevity and even among the opinions of the breeders themselves. Breeding dogs is a long-term, highly selective process, always done with both eyes on the breed standard, which is the blueprint of each purebred dog breed.

After contacting a breeder who may have a dog for you, the next step is to make an appointment to visit the breeder's kennel. You should meet several of the breeder's dogs in addition to the one available for adoption. If logistically possible, you may want to visit several breeders. Remember to make appointments first, and never under any circumstances go directly from one kennel to another. The possibility of carrying disease or parasites on your shoes and clothes from one kennel to another is very real. Even though these things will not affect you,

they will certainly affect the dogs and will cause problems for the breeders. If you want to see many dogs and meet several breeders all at one time, visit a nearby dog show.

It's important that all members of the household go on the kennel visit(s). The breeder will note the dog's reaction to your family and the reaction of each member of the family to the dog. A good breeder can spot potential problems quickly. If the breeder sees warning signals, it may simply result in a feeling that this particular dog is not the right one for you. It could even go so far as to indicate that this breed is not the one you should be considering. The breeder is being honest and helpful. Don't take it personally.

If all works out and the breeder decides that you are the right home for his dog, you will need to discuss the financial arrangements. These need to be discussed and settled before going any further. One of the first requirements of any form of adoption is that the dog be spayed or neutered. If this has not already been taken care of, the breeder may prefer to have his vet do it, asking you to pay for it as partial (or even full) payment for the dog. Most likely, the fee for an adult dog will be less than the fee for a pup.

You will receive the dog's health records, so you'll know when immunizations, including rabies, were given and which ones, if any, the dog will need when you take him to your vet for an initial visit. The breeder may (proudly!) give you a copy of the dog's pedigree. (Try to be impressed, even if it looks totally incomprehensible.) The AKC registration may or may not be transferred over to you; if it is not, you still have the opportunity to apply for the AKC's Indefinite Listing Privilege (ILP).

Dutch, a Portuguese Water Dog with what is known in the breed as "IC" (improper coat), was considered a "throw-away dog" by his breeder, who gave him away for free…an ironic situation when you consider that under the atypical coat was a "wonderdog" in disguise. Dutch is pictured here participating in a water trial and posing in his FEMA search and rescue uniform. Dutch was one of the invaluable canine workers at Ground Zero after the 9/11 tragedy and he also has won high honors competing in performance events and at the PWD national specialty shows.

You will also be made to fully understand that if the adoption does not work out for any reason whatsoever, at any time in the dog's life, the

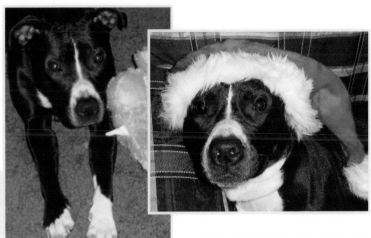

Misty was the last pup left in a litter that resulted from someone's breeding two of his pet dogs. A friend of the "breeder" adopted her at around six months old, and she has flourished into an affectionate, playful dog that exudes happiness and the joy of life.

THE FRIENDLY ADOPTION

Another form of rehoming is taking on a dog that you already know. This is a dog that may have belonged to a friend, neighbor or relative who, due to a move, illness, divorce, death in the family or other circumstance, can no longer keep him. It can be a super arrangement for everyone, especially for the dog. In most cases, nothing more than the dog and his personal possessions are handed over, although it's a good idea to get the transfer in writing. The best part is that you know the dog and he knows you.

dog must be returned to the breeder. The entire transaction should be written out and must cover all of these and any other specific details and limitations. Both parties, the breeder and the adopter, must sign and keep a copy of the adoption agreement.

In this type of adoption, the adjustments will be relatively minimal for both of you, but don't be surprised if after a couple of weeks the dog begins to exhibit unusual behavior. He may walk around the house whining, he may ask to be taken out at odd times (maybe even bringing you his leash, clever dog!) or he may even begin howling in the middle of the night. Perhaps you've guessed it—Rufus is homesick. He's saying in the only way he knows how, "It's been great visiting with you. You're really nice people, but now I want to go home—and I want to go home now!"

Don't coddle the dog and tell him "It's okay." It will take a bit of time for everything to be okay. He has to learn that your home is now his home. He does not need to be babied; what he needs are distractions, which include playing games (catch, chase me, find-the-treat), new toys and, the very best cure of all, new places to be taken for walks. He needs the meandering "sniff-n-smell" kind of walks. Take him to a park, along a river, beside a lake, on a hiking trail, anywhere with new smells, sights and sounds. The good earth is a powerful distraction for a homesick dog.

THE INHERITED DOG

Taking in an inherited dog is a different kind of adoption, with complex problems and solutions. The inherited pet is one that comes to you upon the death of his owner, someone who was either your relative or friend. Let's hope that you were prepared for the inheritance.

Both you and the dog may be mourning the loss of his owner. The dog will probably be devastated and confused. Dogs often exhibit mourning reactions such as whimpering, crying, moping about, refusing to eat and not wanting to move from a certain chair or room. Be patient, gentle and understanding. If he exhibits any of these emotions, it's because he has lost his very best friend. It may take time for

Mandie **(LEFT)** and Asia **(RIGHT)** are both rescues. Mandie was abandoned at age nine and a half when her owners felt she was an "inconvenience." This Maltese at one time was not good with other dogs, but now she's one of the "big guys," living with five Rottweilers, including her special friend Asia.

react quite differently. He will sense the confusion in the situation and may become overly aggressive, baring his teeth, snapping and snarling if anyone comes near him. He can't understand what's going on and is frightened. The vet will be able to sedate the dog just enough so you can take care of him. This behavior does not occur often, but it's worth being warned about and knowing how to handle it. In this case, the dog will need lots of quiet one-on-one time with you. Gradually, the dog will relax and gain confidence in your care and will be able to come off the medication.

you to earn his complete trust, even if he already knows you well.

The other side of canine mourning is less common, but quite startling. If no plans were made ahead of time for the dog in the event of the owner's death, and you are unprepared but taking him because no one knows what to do with him, the dog could

When the dog remains in the same house where he lived with his owner, he'll probably adjust quite quickly apart from some signs of stress such as searching for his owner. However, this situation is unlikely; the typical scenario is that the dog is moved to the home of his new owner. In this case, in addition to getting over the death of his owner, the dog has to make all of the same adjustments as any dog being adopted into a new home. At least you, as the new owner, will know exactly why he is upset. It is also advantageous that you and the dog know each other and you are familiar with his background.

Let the dog take his time settling in with you, your family and your home. Even if he has been there before many times, even if you dog-sat him and he stayed with you for a few days, those were just visits. Bring his toys, bedding and food and water dishes; in fact, bring all of his possessions with him so that he has some familiar items to make him feel more comfortable.

Be affectionate and give the dog plenty of attention, but don't try too

hard to get him to play with you. When he invites you to play by bringing you one of his toys, it's a sign that he is accepting you and his new life. He is testing the waters. Heave a big sigh of relief and let him know that you're flattered!

Keep up with his grooming. Dogs, like people, feel

Sadie Jean found herself in a new home at almost nine years of age after her owners divorced. In addition to being a therapy dog and queen of her local Independence Day parade, Sadie is the household "cheerleader," encouraging and refereeing the other hounds at play with her typical Basset howl.

WHERE THERE'S A WILL

Find out whether there are specific instructions regarding the dog in the deceased's will. Ask the executor of the estate to give you any information regarding the dog's care. Don't be surprised to learn that a sum of money has been set aside for the care of the dog, even in the case of someone who lived on a tiny pension. That dog may have been as important to his owner as any next of kin. As a precaution in our money-conscious world, find out how you will receive the funds and get everything in writing.

While we're on the subject, everyone would be well advised to include plans for their pet(s) in their wills. Often these provisions include not only where the dog will live permanently but also what to do with the dog immediately following the owner's death. The names, addresses and phone numbers of people who can provide this crucial care should be listed. The owner should also include information about the dog's veterinarian, boarding kennel and groomer (the latter two where applicable), and whether or not the dog is on a special diet or any medication. It's not foolish or sentimental to include little things that will help the dog in his change of ownership, things like words or commands the dog knows, daily rituals for bedtime or walks and anything the dog really does or does not like. These small, thoughtful additions will be appreciated in a big way by both your dog and his new caretaker.

better when they are neat and clean. The handling, brushing, stroking and soft talking of a grooming session have therapeutic effects on a dog. Don't forget to go for regular walks. It's amazing what a healing effect walks have on dogs. Dogs do indeed function on sight, smell and sound, all of which they get on nice stop-and-go kinds of walks.

A dog that shared his home with other pets will be less stressed if they all remain together. Even if that can't be the permanent arrangement, it will be easier for the animals if they can stay together for a short time. It's not always possible, but well worth a try. On the other hand, if you are bringing the dog into your home and you have other pets, be alert to possible aggression. The "bone of contention" is not an idle phrase. Any toy could serve as the proverbial bone. Put all toys away for at least a few days until the pets work out their territory, their order in the pack and their status in the human family. You may find yourself walking a tightrope between trying to be gentle and understanding to your inherited dog and being firm, but fair, to your other pets. One way is to keep your hands off, literally, and keep from petting any of them for several days until they have sorted things out.

If you have cats and the new dog is not familiar with cats, put him in his crate (or at very least on his leash) and let the cats investigate their "intruder" while the dog is restrained. Whatever you do, do not hold a cat while introducing her to a dog! One wag of the dog's friendly tail and you could be badly scratched.

SURPRISE!

Still another way to end up with a dog is through your children. Perhaps the dog next door has had a surprise litter of pups and your darling son or daughter comes home cuddling a warm puppy in the time-honored tradition of child-dog conspiracies. "He followed me home, Mom!" What to do?

Well, first off, you are not obligated to keep the pup, regardless of what your child is saying and regardless of your friendship with the neighbor. If you can't meet the demands that a puppy will make on your time and finances, plus commit to training and care for the dog's entire life (think 15 years…yes, that's years, not minutes, hours or weeks), return the puppy immediately and promise the kids something else on their wish list.

A puppy is not a spur-of-the-moment fun item for the kids to play with over the weekend or during summer vacation. They haven't brought home a cute toy that will sit on the shelf when they tire of it. A dog's needs have to be taken care of from sun-up until bedtime every single day—including weekends, vacations and holidays—for 10 to 15 years, possibly even longer. When the time is right to add a dog to your home, your investment in care pays off in the fun and companionship of owning a dog.

Hallie was a lost dog but luckily was reunited with her owners thanks to proper ID. Her "finders" kept her overnight while her owners were located, and in that short time the sweet terrier mix made a lasting impression on everyone who met her.

LOST, BUT NOT LEAST

A lost dog enters your life, perhaps scratching at your door or caught in your headlights wandering along a dark road. How did this dog become lost in the first place? The lack of a well-maintained fence is a major cause. Or perhaps he got away when his leash broke, or he jumped out of the car when the door opened, or he ran through a gate that someone forgot to close or he made an escape through a door left open by the kids when they went out to play. No matter how it came about, the dog got out of his customary boundaries and just kept going. Such escapes can be frightening, even for an otherwise self-assured dog.

Senior dogs who become lost have additional problems. They may suffer from dementia, dimmed eyesight, diminished hearing or some loss of scent discrimination. They are disoriented easily and in no time become completely lost. Sometimes a senior dog will be found standing in the middle of a street, completely confused; this is both frightening and dangerous for the dog. An older dog needs a careful, watchful owner.

Lost dogs can turn up many miles from home as they wander and cross town lines. In an urban area, turning a corner at the end of his street could be all a dog needs to become scared and lost. A prime example of this occurs in bad weather, particularly during thunderstorms. Thunder is a natural signal to all animals to run for cover and can cause a dog to panic, take off and become lost even quite close to home.

How to Approach a Lost Dog

No matter how he became lost, a lost dog tends to be frightened and cautious of strangers. If he didn't come knocking at your door, and you've spotted him on the street or in a parking lot, approach with care. If he seems scared, don't walk directly toward him and don't, whatever you do, try to chase him. Kneel or crouch down and keep up a low, calm, reassuring line of comforting words: "Good dog…here boy…what a good dog… come on fellow." It can be frustrating because most lost dogs are really terrified and won't come near people who are trying to help them.

If you happen to have food with you, gently toss a couple of small bits toward the dog. If he takes one, toss a few more bits slightly closer to you. As he gets near, offer your open hand with the food in it. Then comes the trickiest part of all. If he has a collar, you can slip one hand quickly (but gently) through it while the dog is eating out of your other hand. If there is no collar, or you can't see it under the fur, you can attempt to grab him securely by the scruff of the neck so he can't turn and bite you. But, obviously, you should only do this if it's a small and/or manageable dog and you can quickly hold him firmly with your other hand beneath his chest.

If you came on the scene prepared, you'll have a leash with you. The dog may, just possibly, associate the sight of the leash with happy walks and he'll come toward you (but don't count on it!). Make a noose by pulling the end of the leash up through the loop of the handle and, at the appropriate moment, slip it over the dog's head. All of your movements need to be calm and your voice low and steady.

If none of this is possible, try to keep the dog in sight and get help as quickly as possible. A cell phone to the rescue! Merely reporting where and when you saw a lost dog can help in his being found and picked up.

Above all else, remember that frightened dogs do bite! Small, sweet-looking, fluffy dogs and big, tough-looking dogs alike all bite when they are scared or doubtful about trusting a stranger. If you are by yourself, don't ever attempt to handle any dog that has been injured and is in pain, as the dog is almost certain to bite. Another perfect moment for a cell phone! Stay with the dog and call for professional help.

What's Next?

Now let's say you've got him. A lost dog comes to you, the finder, with a bunch of questions. First of all, if you found him, who lost him? Where did he come from? What do you do with him? If he has an ID tag or a town license tag, or was tattooed or microchipped, you have just found one very lucky dog. If there's a phone number on the ID tag, call it. It's probably his home. If he only has a town license tag, call the animal-control officer or police department of that town to report your find. In small towns or after hours, it could very well be the police

LOST AND FOUND

A very considerate and grateful owner, upon finding his dog well taken care of, would offer some financial compensation. Technically, though, he is not obligated to offer anything but his gratitude. If you did not have to spend much for the dog's care, this is your moment to be a super do-gooder by suggesting that any reward money be given to a non-profit canine charity such as a local spay-neuter clinic or rescue group, or an organization like the American Kennel Club's Canine Health Foundation. In fact, making that suggestion just might prompt a reward where none had been considered before.

This affectionate but underweight Boston Terrier/pit bull mix was found huddled under a guardrail on a busy New Jersey highway. She was picked up by a passerby who noticed her on the side of the road and was brought to a local shelter, where she was not reclaimed and so awaits adoption.

department that will handle your call. If the dog has not been reported missing locally, you might also contact the dog wardens in neighboring towns.

Provide as much identification (color, size, possible breed, etc.) as you can, including a tattoo number if you can read it. A tattoo may be inside the flap of the dog's ear, in the groin area or inside a rear leg; in other words, in a spot where there is likely to be the least amount of hair so that the tattoo is visible.

While a microchip can only be read with a special scanner, many animal-control officers and veterinarians now have this tool. Further, if the dog is microchipped, he may be wearing a tag with the phone number of the

FACING PAGE: Doberman Muzzy was picked up as a stray and was 20 pounds underweight. She awaited adoption in a local animal shelter and was adopted by an owner who helped her get healthy and develop her many talents: Muzzy has titles in obedience and rally competition, has her Canine Good Citizen certification and is certified with Therapy Dogs International.

microchip registry and his chip ID number so that someone can call the registry and try to get his information that way. However, tags can become detached from collars, so lost dogs as a rule should be scanned for a chip if possible, tag or no tag.

If there is no identification at all on the dog, or if the dog does have ID but you have not been able to locate the owners, the local animal-control officer will likely pick up the dog and take him to the pound. Hopefully, once the owners realize that they have lost their dog, they will contact the shelters, pounds and police in their town and surrounding towns.

If the dog has contact information on his tag, the shelter workers will keep trying to get in touch with the owners. If the dog has a town license, the animal-control officer can likely trace the license back to the dog's owners. Even if the dog is not wearing a license tag, sometimes the animal-control officer can use the town dog-registration data to determine who may own the dog. Alternatively, if you are able to look after the dog, you may decide to bring him home with you while his owners are looked for.

In addition to doing all of the things that we've discussed, you can check the "lost pets" section in the local newspapers and keep an eye out for "lost dog" posters posted around town or in neighboring towns. If you are able to identify the dog's breed or mix with any degree of certainty or can just give a good description of the dog, call someone in a local dog club, a dog trainer or a nearby veterinarian's

office to alert them that this dog has been found. You might also ask around, as neighbors or other residents in town might have heard of someone's losing his dog.

If nothing turns up in the newspaper after a few days and you have the dog home with you, you could run a

Australian Cattle Dog/black Lab mix Madison was found on the street, where her owners suspect she was born. She is afraid of loud noises and a bit timid, but her owners describe her as a "sweetheart."

"found pet" ad in your local paper. Do not give away too much information. You want the owner to claim the dog, not someone just looking for a free pooch. If your local radio station offers this service, ask them to announce the dog as found. Needless to say, you should also listen for their reports of dogs that are lost. You should also call the local police departments and shelters to see if anyone has called to report their dog as missing.

If, after a period of time, nothing brings forth the dog's owner, you may decide to keep him. By now he has no doubt hunkered down and decided to accept your fine food and generous hospitality. Just remember that if the owner turns up some months from now and can positively identify the dog, you'll have to give him up. That's often the law.

On the other hand, if no one shows up and you cannot keep the dog long-term, contact local rescue groups and no-kill shelters. If none of these has room for the dog and you are considering your town's shelter or pound, acquaint yourself with their regulations and check out their facilities before turning the dog over. As previously mentioned, some shelters and pounds have a no-kill policy, but others are overwhelmed with strays and will only keep animals for a specified number of days before euthanizing them. This is particularly true in large cities and very rural areas. Further, some municipal pounds are reasonably well funded and thus are well run, while some struggle to stay open and offer only the most basic shelter and food. If your local dog pound doesn't come close to your minimum standards, a veterinarian's office is a good source for locating a well-run rescue or private shelter, as many vets today work with shelters and rescue volunteers. Be prepared, as you likely will be asked to make a donation when you turn over the dog.

If you cannot find adequate accommodations for the dog, where he will be cared for and safe while

Senior rescue dogs Skeeter (Basset Hound) and Sanders (Basset/Lab mix) were both found and both had major health problems. Skeeter eventually had both eyes removed but is now otherwise healthy. Sanders recovered from parasite infestation and mange, but still copes with hip dysplasia and a fused spine. Both of these special-needs dogs are sweet and affectionate, with so much to give. Their owner can't say enough glowing things about her boys!

awaiting a new permanent home, you might reconsider and be able to hold on to him a little longer until a good situation comes along.

Rescued Bullmastiff Leo's arrival is
eagerly anticipated by Nick, another
rescued Bullmastiff and self-appointed
welcoming committee.

CHAPTER 7

Your Adopted Dog's Homecoming

Few people are given the opportunity to start life all over again. The rescued dog is given that chance when you open your home and heart to him. Whether he chose you or you chose him, how you care for this dog is vital to setting up a long-lasting companionable relationship. A well-meaning adopter goes wrong when he believes that a newly adopted dog only needs food and lots of love to become the pet of his dreams. When a dog is returned to a rescue, breeder or shelter, complaints all too often sound something like: "We showered this dog with love, but he just doesn't love us."

We have no idea how a dog perceives the human emotion we call love, but we do know that trust—the ability to trust and to be trusted—is a basic factor in a dog's life. Trust from a dog builds slowly and we must earn it. It's the result of fairness, consistency and good discipline. Without trust there can be no companionship, no reliability, no easy way to teach acceptable behavior or to eliminate behavioral problems. A medieval meaning of the word "trust" was "faithful," and that's a word we use as high praise of our favorite dogs.

PREPARATIONS

The first thing you'll need is plenty of time. Plan to pick up your dog when the family will be at home. In a working household, it could be just before a long holiday weekend or, even better, at the start of a week or two of vacation time. He needs to know whose dog he is, especially if he has been no one's dog. Give him a name and use it every time you look at him or speak to him. Use lots of "good dog" praise and don't overuse "no."

Preparing your home for any new dog, of any age, of any breed or mix comes down to one word: safety. This means safety of the dog, safety of the family and safety of your worldly possessions. You can prevent accidents if you are fully aware of potential dangers. For the dog, the more obvious dangers are things such as any door that opens onto the street or an unfenced area, or one that leads out of an apartment into a public hallway.

Kitchen garbage, trash cans and wastepaper baskets need to be kept completely out of the dog's reach. If the spaghetti in today's garbage doesn't entice him, tomorrow's leftovers will. Toys and clothes left lying around are fair game for destruction by a playful or bored dog, which means that your belongings are ruined and he is ingesting things that could cause him harm. But here's a positive slant on things: having a new dog in the house will teach everyone in the family to put their things away.

Household cleaners must be put inside kitchen cabinets after every use, and all forms of medication kept behind the closed door of the medicine cabinet. Read labels. Garden supplies such as weed killers and fertilizers come with "hazardous to your health" warnings, and that includes the dog's health. All automobile products (especially antifreeze, which is lethal to animals) and other chemicals kept in the garage must be moved onto shelves higher than the dog can reach when standing on his hind legs.

Maybe you've taken all of these precautions already because you have young kids or you previously had a dog. Great! You're ahead of the game. But double check, just to be sure, and keep reminding everyone in the family that this is a new dog. You don't know what he might get into.

a level playing field, but one that could be full of surprises. You may discover that he loves the UPS man, but will send up a barrage of barking to protect you from the garbage man. (Actually, those are common canine reactions. The UPS man brings stuff. To the dog, that's good. The trash collector takes things away. That's bad. The dog is

THE WELCOME MAT

You've bought a nice new collar and leash, food and water bowls, a crate and/or cushy bed and some appropriate toys and now you're all set to bring Barney home. You don't know this dog very well and may not even know very much about him, only what you've been told. You don't even speak the same language. Relax. He doesn't know anything about you either. That makes for

Bullmastiff Sadie has made a promise to her owner always to try to see eye to eye with him and always to share her toys.

Doing what Bassets do best, Hugh snuggles up with his dad. Hugh's owners met him at a rescue group's adoption event at their local pet-supply store, and it was mutual love at first sight.

always want him to eliminate. Stand with him while he sniffs around and makes up his mind to go along with your choice. (We will discuss potty training in more detail later.) After the potty pit-stop, you can begin the grand tour.

Walk in the door with this new dog on leash, regardless of his age or size. If you let him race in all by himself, the first thing he will do is lift a leg on your new couch to mark it as "his" territory (females squat and ruin carpets). This is not the time for freedom. It's time to take Barney on a guided tour of the house. As you take him slowly through each room of his new home, say "Good dog" when he does anything of which you approve. For example, he sniffs the couch but doesn't attempt to jump

only protecting your trash from being stolen!)

Remember you are starting at square one and the teaching/learning program begins immediately. The first thing you should do upon bringing your new dog home is to take him, on leash, to the limited area where you will up (or lift a leg); that earns a "Good dog." Try not to say "No" to everything he goes near that he shouldn't. Instead, use a guttural-sounding "uh-uh" or "aach" as you guide him away (that's why he's on leash and he's "guided away," not choked). These sounds are closer to doggy lingo and he may have heard "No" so many times in his previous home that it has ceased to have any meaning.

If Barney will be allowed upstairs, take him—still on leash—and pay close attention to how he manages the stairs, especially coming down. An older dog's hips and joints may not be as agile as they once were. A puppy, on the other hand, might try a flying leap from the top! Or he may never have seen a staircase before. A little guidance or reassurance may be necessary. Watch him also if you have any outside steps. In bedrooms, correct any attempted jump onto beds with "Off! Good dog."

Take him to the room where he'll be confined at night and whenever he must be left alone. Show him his bed and/or crate and toss a dog biscuit into it so he'll know it's definitely his. As he goes for the biscuit, you can get in a "Good dog" (or "Good bed"). Put his water

CORRECTING YOUR DOG CORRECTLY

What if Barney misbehaves and doesn't immediately hit the road to his den? If you caught him in the act of misbehaving, give him a one-word verbal correction before putting him somewhere other than his crate (such as a safe, dog-proofed room) before you lose your patience. Then stop and think why the misbehavior occurred, why no one was watching the dog and how the incident could have been prevented. If he had a potty accident, got into the garbage or otherwise made a mess, clean it up and move on. By the time you are finished, Barney will have completely forgotten the incident (timing is one of the important "T" words in training!). Let him back out into the family area…remembering to keep an eye on him this time.

bowl down where you intend to keep it. The food dish will go next to it at dinnertime. Spend a little more time in this room so he can become familiar with it. If it's the kitchen, and there's a pet gate in the doorway, let Barney off leash and treat yourself to a coffee break. You've earned it!

Zelda is a Flat-Coated Retriever mix whose bright smile matches her happy-go-lucky personality. She was rescued by her forever family from a shelter in central New Jersey.

The house tour is over. He may be exhausted from all the excitement or he may be keyed up. A new home, a new family, a new life—this is heady stuff! If you have nothing special in mind and Barney is in high gear, looking for more action, give him some outdoor exercise: chasing a toy or retrieving a ball if you have a fenced yard, or a short walk on leash if not. A doggie inspection of your backyard is best done on leash if there are areas such as flower beds or bushes where leg-lifting or digging is forbidden.

If he seems relaxed, the leash comes off and you can settle into whatever is normal for you and the family at this time of day, but only where someone can keep an eye on the dog. If that means sitting around watching baseball on TV or reading the paper, give Barney a chew toy and watch him to be sure that he doesn't sink his teeth into a chair leg or the rug for his chewing pleasure.

Barney is not yet sure what's expected of him. Exposing him to the normal routine in your home will let him begin to accustom himself to the scents, sounds and actions of his new family. It will also let you see his response to it all. Be prepared for his often amusing reactions. He may bark at your cell phone, cringe at the dishwasher or cock his head in puzzlement at the microwave. These may be all totally new, foreign sounds to him and you can only wonder why. He will need help in unlearning any reactions you find undesirable. Gradually he'll learn what's okay (and what is not okay) in his new home. It's a big job and it will take time. Be patient. He's trying.

THE CRATE

Unless this lucky dog is a true giant and you don't have room for a large-enough crate, a crate makes the best sleeping quarters. The crate gives your dog a den/bed of his very own, which he will like, and you'll like it, too. Here are a few very basic rules for you to follow:

- You will never make your dog go into his crate as punishment.
- At night the crate door will be closed; the rest of the time, it will be left open so he can enter and exit his crate as he pleases.
- The crate is out of bounds to all kids.

Your pet-supply store should have a wide array of crates in different sizes and types, such as the closed plastic or fiberglass type and the more open wire type. A properly sized crate will allow your adult dog to fully stand, lie down and turn around. Crate pads are available, or an old bathmat or folded cotton blanket will do nicely. A cover (or towel) over the wire crate at night makes it a snug sleeping den. Put the crate where it will be away from drafts, vents and air-conditioning and heating units.

After a six-hour ride from a kill shelter to his foster home, Newman is exhausted. He was adopted by a retired couple who renamed him Fido and call him "the love of their lives."

interactive, and even food and water bowls are shared to some extent (when empty, you refill them). The crate, however, is the ultimate in canine personal property.

That is also why Barney is never—never ever—put into his crate as punishment. A clever dog will high-tail it into his crate when he hears an angry voice. He is not ashamed of what he did, nor is he sorry about it. He's one smart dog, heading for the safety of his den to get out of your way! It's impor-tant to understand his behavior. Many dogs come into rescue not because they were mistreated but because they were mishandled or misunderstood.

A bonus use of the crate comes when you visit friends and relatives or travel anywhere. A dog that is accustomed to spending time in a crate will be much more

Children in the family should be told that the "dog's den" is his and his alone. They must never, ever even pretend to enter the crate. Many kids who are bitten by family pets have brought it on themselves by trying to invade their dogs' private space. Perfectly calm, sweet dogs can be very possessive about their crates or beds. Toys are welcome than one that chases Aunt Mary's cat around the house. The majority of motels and hotels that accept pets will only allow dogs in the room if they are crated. This rule prevents damage to the room (which you'd have to pay for) and also considers that the room's next occupants may be allergic to dog hair. Another plus of the crate is that in the car the crate is the dog's best safety belt. (For a large dog, use a gate-type safety barrier to keep him in the back of the car.)

VETERINARY VISIT

Regardless of when your rescue dog was last checked by a vet, it's best to have an appointment scheduled with the veterinarian you will use before picking up the dog. If nothing else, it allows the dog and the vet to meet, but there are probably also questions you will want to ask regarding the dog's food, his weight, the amount and type of exercise he should be getting and his overall physical condition and care. If the dog's age is unknown or estimated, you might ask the vet's opinion on this as well.

On her way to her new home is Dharma, a lucky Shiba Inu adopted from a breed rescue.

A well-trained dog is a fun companion who can accompany his owners anywhere. Piccolo Bello participates in most of his family's activities, and kayaking is one of his favorites.

CHAPTER 8

Learning the Routine

HOUSE-TRAINING

You'll have to agree that "house-training" sounds much better than "housebreaking" when it relates to a new dog in your home. After all, "training" is teaching the dog; "breaking" doesn't sound all that nice. Keep in mind that the rescue dog is under double pressure while adjusting to his new home. He is unlearning his old ways and at the same time having to relearn how to do everything your way. The rules of house-training will vary slightly depending on how the dog arrived on your doorstep. We'll begin with discussing the adult dog from a rescue group or the older dog rehomed from a breeder.

Maybe you were told that your newly adopted dog is house-trained. That is only partially true. He may have been house-trained in his previous home, but now he has to be house-trained to your house, your schedule and your selection of where he goes potty. You also have to learn to recognize how he lets you know when he needs to go. So your job is both to acquaint him with the new routine and to watch for his "gotta go" signals!

One big benefit of getting an older dog is that he will not need to eliminate as often as a young puppy would. A true senior canine citizen, or one with special needs, however, may be on a more frequent potty schedule, like that of a puppy. It's also a well-known fact that it is generally harder to house-train toy breeds because they are so close to the floor. If you have a very small dog, maintain a tight schedule with frequent on-leash trips to the potty area and be constantly alert for his signals until you both have your routine all worked out.

The Importance of a Schedule

Your adopted dog may be a young puppy, he may be an adult who was not house-trained as a puppy, he may be used to life as a "kennel dog" or he may just need a refresher course in his new home. Whatever the case, there is no reason why you should not be able to house-train him. If he was a kennel dog, you will have to find out what he is used to regarding his toileting habits. Kennels are run on fairly precise schedules, so find out when he was let out throughout the day, when he was fed and when he went out for his last nightly bath-room trip before bedtime. (Write it all down so you

don't forget!) The fact that the dog is now in a totally different environment is in your favor. He'll be taking notes of when and how each member of your family does what. Help him by sticking to a routine.

Regardless of age, type or size, every dog in a new home needs to be main-tained on a fixed schedule, starting with being taken out on leash every two or three hours. This is not so much for the dog's benefit as for yours. Keep track of when he does what, and after a week or so you'll know how often he really does need to go potty and you can cut back on the number of trips. Just don't cut back too soon. Give him time to adjust.

Taking the dog out on leash for his potty breaks is vital to successful house-training. These are not walks; they are business trips. The reason for the leash is to keep the dog's mind on doing his "business" while you keep him in one relatively small area, moving him back and forth if he decides to sit and look at you. (The only exception to the leash rule would be if you have a kennel run that you want him to use; in this case, you must stay with him until he eliminates.) If you will walk your dog in the neighborhood for his potty trips, be sure to curb your dog and pick up after him! This is not just courteous; it's also the law in most places.

No matter where you take him, you must be right there as he eliminates to say "Good dog." Timing is a key word in training. Remember it. Two seconds after the dog has eliminated is too late for praise. By then he's scuffing up turf or enjoying a total body shake, and that is not what you want to praise him for!

Don't interrupt the business at hand with ecstatic praise or treats. Your calm verbal approval is enough. Save treat rewards for when he obeys something like a "Come" command. Going potty is merely answering nature's call. Where he does it (where you take him on leash) and when he does it (when you take him or when he asks to go out) is what

"Is it time to go out yet?"

Jade knows that a sturdy every-day collar with proper ID tags is a must-have in every well-dressed dog's wardrobe.

you are praising. So here are the basics: On schedule. On leash. "Good dog." Good timing...there's your T word again. Simple! After any successful trip to his potty spot would be a good time for a walk. If you're already out on a walk, you can continue on a longer walk or bring him home for some playtime.

Watch It!

If everyone in the family is alert to the dog's scratching or staring at the door, or his circling or whining signals, there should be no potty accidents. If an accident does occur, figure that it's your fault, not the dog's. He's giving you the signals, but you may still have a problem with his language. Remember the "T" word: timing! If you catch him in the act, shout "aaagh" and take him outside pronto. Two seconds after he has finished is too late. There's no punishment, no harsh words. Put him in another room (not in his crate) and clean the area using a cleanser/deodorizer made especially for pet clean-ups. If the scent remains, a dog's acute sense of smell will lure him back to the same place to eliminate. Outdoors, that's a plus, but you don't want that happening in the house. Regular household cleansers will not get rid of the scent.

Accidents followed by punishments only lead to behavioral problems and are easily avoided. Don't relax on your end of the deal because the dog is six years old and

has been perfect for two days. Remember to stick to a schedule, watch for signals and give everyone, especially Barney, time to adjust.

FEED ME!

If your new friend came from the dog pound, consider upgrading the quality of his food; check with your vet for suggestions. It's best to change to a new food slowly, over a period of a week or so, to avoid tummy upsets. Find out what he was being

"T" FOR TWO

Perhaps the most important "T" word in training is timing, no matter what you are doing with your dog. Whether house-training, teaching commands or giving corrections, you must be sharp with your cue words and praise. Dogs think in the present, so timing is the key to communicating properly with your dog. For example, if you tell your dog to "Sit" and he sits, and then you tell him "Good dog" after he stands up, he will think he's being praised for standing up. If your dog chews up one of your shoes, and you find the shoe an hour later and tell him "No," he will have no idea what he did wrong. So always remember the big "T" in training: timing.

fed previously and give him a mixture of the old food and new food. Gradually decrease the amount of old food and increase the amount of the new food, so that eventually his food portion consists entirely of the new food. In addition to being caused by a sudden change in food, diarrhea also can result from the stress of a new environment and/or a change in water.

Most dogs do best on two meals a day: a small one in the morning and a larger one in late afternoon or early evening. If you were not told when and how much your new dog is used to being fed, follow the directions on the food package for the size and age of your dog, and be sure to discuss the dog's diet with the vet at that first appointment. Mixing dry food with a bit of canned food is the way that most dogs like their meals.

Some dogs are put on what is called a "self-feeding" or "free-feeding" schedule. If Barney is used to this type of feeding routine, it's up to you whether you want to continue with it or whether you want to give him regularly scheduled meals. There are drawbacks to self-feeding. For example, what goes in must come out, and if he's nibbling away at food all day it will be more diffi-

Tosha had barely any hair and weighed only 1.5 pounds when she was rescued by her caring owners. Today, this sweet and affectionate girl is a 4-pound 6-ounce beauty who happily shares her home with the other rescued pets that her animal-loving family has saved.

cult to schedule potty breaks. Self-feeding can also contribute to obesity. He does not need food available to him all day; a dog won't starve between morning and evening dinner times!

Scheduled feeding times also give you the opportunity to do a little training for good manners. Dinner's ready, so ask for a nice "Sit" before putting his dish on the floor. If he hasn't a clue what you mean by "Sit," you will have to show him. Hold the dish in front of the dog and over his head and, with the other hand, gently press down on his rear. As you lean over, your hand with the dish will almost automatically move back over the dog's head and, as he looks up and his rear goes down, he will sit. As he sits (remember your "T" word!), say "Good sit" and put the dish on the floor.

If you feed him prior to your own evening meal, Barney will be somewhat more inclined to leave you alone while you're eating. Only "somewhat." Much depends on his previous environment. In a kennel or shelter (or scavenging) he didn't have the opportunity to beg at the dinner table. The smell of food may bring on a "share and share alike" attitude.

On the other hand, his previous family may have thought it was cute to offer tidbits from their plates. Enforce your rules according to how you feel about it. And stick to the rules. (Kids, too!) Dogs are creatures of habit. If you don't take advantage of it, they will!

BEDTIME

You don't know your new dog too well yet, so it would definitely not be smart to let him sleep on anyone's bed. He needs a place of his own, either a crate or a dog bed in a confined safe (i.e., dog-proofed) area such as the kitchen. If he is not crated, a pet gate blocking the doorway is always better than a closed door. Being shut in by a solid door is an invitation for destruction,

"Dog bed? What's a dog bed?"
Bullmastiff Marty has decided
that what's good enough
for his owners…

preceded by barking, howling and whining, if he panics. If he can see through to another room, he can relax. A dim nightlight (above the kitchen counter) helps, too.

After you take him out for his last potty trip, put him in his crate or bed with a good-night biscuit. Shut the crate door, turn out the lights and ignore any crying or fussing. If you respond in any way— in any way at all—picture the dog saying smugly to himself, "Ha! I gotcha!" He will resume his fussing until you respond again. This "game" could go on all night!

At least for the first week or two, all family members should avoid midnight raids on the kitchen. Barney may not understand and may think that the activity means it's time to get up, or he may try to assist in the raid.

First thing in the morning, when you are ready, let him out of the crate, snap on his leash and take him to the spot where you want him to relieve himself. It will be a week or more (maybe four!) before you can just open the door and let him out into his fenced-in yard all by himself. Mornings in many households are a bit hectic, so when he's done his job and you bring him in, give him a dog biscuit in his bed or crate (door open) to keep him happy until his breakfast is ready.

THE DAILY SCHEDULE

If none of the family members are at home during the day on weekdays you will have to make provisions for your dog. If you adopted your dog from a rescue group, hopefully you were matched up with a dog who is accustomed to a working schedule. A dog from the pound or animal shelter will need more time and more patience on your part before he understands that you will return.

After breakfast and before you leave for work, take the dog for as long a walk as you can, in addition to another potty stop. When you go out, you will leave Barney confined to one area or room where he can't do any damage and where he cannot get into anything that could harm him. That is very, very important. Giving him

The daily routine in this house allows for plenty of time spent with the dogs at the end of the workday.

freedom of the house only means freedom for Barney to either get into danger or get into trouble and then be punished. That's neither safe nor fair to him.

Have his area prepared ahead of time. Check to see that all electrical cords, small appliances, etc., are out of his reach. Leave his crate door open, and you might also provide him with a soft dog bed elsewhere in the room. Out of reach, or in another room, leave a radio on low (a dog's normal hearing is excellent), tuned to an easy-listening station so there will be intermittent music and voices. It's not to entertain him, but to provide a mix of background sounds so he won't go into a barking frenzy at every little noise he hears. Your neighbors will appreciate your thoughtfulness.

Be sure that he has enough fresh water and a couple of safe toys. One or two small dog biscuits would also be appreciated. (Don't be surprised if he saves them until you get home. He's not taking any

chances on starving if you don't return by dinnertime.)

Actually leaving the house is the hard part for most dog owners. The last person out the door says, "'Bye, Barney." Period. That's it. End of the goodbye scene. Dragging out the farewell with hugs, pats, cuddles and sweet talk about when you'll be back and how sorry you are to leave is only upsetting to the dog. It will also bring out the "con artist" in him and he'll play on your heartstrings, begging you not to go. So, keep it to a quick goodbye and leave!

Don't be surprised if he has picked up on your impending departure—the shoes that are not your "dog walking" ones, clothes that you don't wear on weekends, picking up the car keys, patting your wallet pocket, reaching for your coat—all of those things register with a dog. He knows you're going, so go!

The first person to arrive home is the delegated

"go-potty" person. Then, after Barney has relieved himself, it's time for some physical activity such as a nice brisk walk or some energetic playtime in the backyard. That's what the rescue volunteers were referring to when they asked if you were able to give this dog his much-needed exercise. The types of exercise and the length of the activity sessions depend on the age and health of the dog.

Weekends are when you make up for lost time and get in some extra fun and games. A leisurely stroll in the park, a trip to the beach, a hike in the woods—anything new, different and stimulating to Barney will be a perfect means of bonding with your newfound friend. Go for walks that are attuned to the dog—the stop-and-sniff kind of walks. Cardiovascular jaunts may be great for you and fine if that's all you have time for first thing in the morning or during the week. The weekend walks are different. These walks are centered around Barney, not on getting him out and back in a hurry so you can rush off to work. Like all dogs, he will want to investigate (via scent) everything en route, with plenty of leg-lifts or squats to say, "I, Barney, was here."

It was instant love for Black and Tan Coonhound Andy, who was adopted from breed rescue by a family who said that they "felt like he had been their dog forever" after just a few days.

Competition is not just for purebreds! Mixed-breed rescue dog Meghan competes and has earned various titles in agility trials held by several organizations including the United States Dog Agility Association and the North American Dog Agility Council.

THE NEED FOR OBEDIENCE

If you don't know much or anything about your new dog's previous training, it's not too hard to find out. Tell him (with a smile; this is not boot camp) to "Sit," "Come," "Stay" or, when you're out for a walk, "Heel." If he does any one of them, no matter how well, you'll know he has had some training. But you'll never know how he was trained and whether he enjoyed his lessons or found them to be a dreaded ordeal. This time around, you're going to make it fun for both of you.

No matter how well or how poorly Barney responded to your "test" commands, you should enroll in a six- or eight-week basic obedience course. This will help cement the bond between you while letting you observe his social skills (or lack of them) with other dogs and people. Training classes establish you and your dog as a team so, even in a group, he will look to you for what "we" are going to do next.

Barney may be totally illiterate in social graces as well as obedience, so you need to show him how proud you are of every little thing he gets right. Keep it super-friendly. There's no need for harsh corrections. If he doesn't respond correctly, it's only because he didn't understand what you asked him to do. Remember the "T" word for timing. Praise him as he does the right thing.

A dog that suffered through previous training with rough physical corrections and angry words may be defensive about the whole idea. An excellent way to overcome his attitude is to use a head collar rather than the usual chain (choke) training collar. Guiding him calmly by his head instead of jerking on his neck could easily make the difference between success and failure in your training efforts. A head collar is similar to a horse's bridle and is definitely not a muzzle. Barney can yawn, pant and gobble the occasional treat while wearing his head collar.

At home, break up practice sessions with playtime. Five or ten minutes may be the extent of his attention span. If he seems bored or just isn't catching on to what you're trying to teach him, you both need time out. End the training session by having him do any one thing you know he does well, then praise and stop. Call it quits for the day and play ball or do any other fun activity.

Once trained in the basics, the sky is the limit with what you can do with your rescue dog. Darby loves to compete in agility, as you can tell by her smile.

Be sure to practice anytime, anywhere—walking from one room to the next is "Heel." A call to dinner is "Come" and "Sit." Pick up the brush for a bit of grooming and it's "Stand." You're the leader, so you go through a door first and it's "Wait." Your whole day can be a practice session, with lots of appropriate (timely) praise for any job well done. All the while you're bonding with each other and building a firm foundation for trust.

GOOD GROOMING BEHAVIOR

No matter his age, breed or mix of breeds, grooming is an important part of your dog's life. It is also strongly tied to obedience. If he was groomed in his previous home, he'll understand what it's all about and appreciate the attention. If he was never groomed before he was rescued, he has a few things to learn. Brushing, combing, trimming his nails so he can walk comfortably, bathing him with a pleasant-smelling doggie shampoo and taking care of his teeth will make him look—and even feel—marvelous, but he may not appreciate the process!

Barney may tell you to mind your own business and keep your hands off. In that case, some good-natured training is in order. Get him up off the ground (that's his level) onto a grooming table, picnic table or work bench and begin with brief daily sessions of casual brushing and lots of calm sweet talk. Surprise him now and then (when he's standing nicely) with a small treat. As he settles down, try adding more grooming. Keep telling him how good he's being. Use his name a lot. Give him the spa treatment.

TIMING AND THE OTHER "T"S

Timing is not the only important "T" word. We also have Teaching, which goes hand in hand with Training. Then of course there is Rufus's favorite "T": Treats! Remember your "T"s and the two of you will be a TEAM!

If you can't get beyond casual brushing, and he's a long-coated or curly-coated dog, have him groomed professionally. Don't put it off, because that will only make it harder for the groomer, and much harder for the dog. Ask the groomer to show you how to brush or comb him routinely to stay one step ahead of mats. Also ask your vet or your groomer how to apply the flea and tick preventive; many of these are "spot-on" treatments applied to an area of the dog's skin.

Maybe your dog is smooth-coated or short-haired, and you figure that you won't have to do much grooming. Wrong! It may surprise you to know that these coats definitely do shed. Daily brushing means less hair on the furniture and all over your clothes. Nails also have to be cut; ears and teeth have to be cleaned.

If you got your dog from a breeder or from breed rescue, ask for breed-specific grooming instruc-tions when you pick up the dog, including a demonstra-tion if possible.

If you are going to do most of the grooming your-self, you'll need to know what tools and supplies to buy. You might want to invest in a grooming table, or you can use another suit-able raised surface. If your dog will be professionally groomed, you need to know how often to make appoint-ments and if there are any special instructions to pass on to the groomer. For exam-ple, some dogs do better on one type of shampoo than another; some dogs go ballistic at the sight of nail clippers or a nail grinder. Basic weekly grooming is a must, no matter what the coat type, so make life easier on yourself by finding out exactly what's involved beforehand.

WALKING THE DOG

It may seem obvious, but the dog's collar and leash need to be the right size and strength for the dog. The

A rescued Rottie does some stretching before a nice walk.

breeder, rescue representative or shelter volunteer can give you advice; failing that, an employee at your pet-supply shop will be able to guide you. For everyday wear the best kind of collar is a buckle collar that fits so you can just slip two fingers beneath it. Just be sure the dog cannot back out of the collar you choose. Another excellent choice is a martingale (or double-loop) collar. The second loop tightens slightly when the dog pulls ahead or lags behind, preventing him from slipping out of the collar.

A training (or choke) collar is exactly that. It is used for training sessions only and then removed. The reason is simple. The loose ring on this type of collar can catch on something and the dog would choke to death trying to struggle free. This is one reason why many trainers now prefer the head collar for training. When you finish an obedience training session, either in class or at home, remove your dog's training collar and leave on his everyday collar, which bears his ID, license and rabies tags. Never put these tags on a training collar.

Now we come to walking the dog. As previously mentioned, taking the dog outside to relieve himself is not a walk. Go for a real walk after he has gone potty (take clean-up bags with you just in case!). Your new-to-you dog will want to sniff everything as you go. It's his only way of learning all about this new neighborhood. People say, "Let's take the dog for a walk," but in this case it's better to say, "Let's let the dog take us for a walk." The dog thinks of it not just as physical exercise but also as a chance to explore, to take in the sights.

This is not to say that unruly on-lead behavior is acceptable; you still have to be the one in charge. You may discover rather quickly that Rufus needs more obedience training than you thought. Pulling you around is not acceptable. Barking or growling at an approaching dog or person is definitely not acceptable. Jumping up on friends or neighbors you meet along the way is not a proper greeting. Keep in mind that any of these things may have been completely tolerated by his previous owners. Head for home and many more positive-reinforcement lessons. Get more help from your obedience instructor.

Kandee, doing what herding dogs do best.

No problems here for Macaroon, a rescued mixed breed, and Dulcy, a Basset Hound adopted from a breed rescue group. These "siblings" enjoy each other's company and are vigilant on their "deck duty" shift.

CHAPTER 9

Problems and Solutions

DEALING WITH PROBLEMS

So far we've been assuming that everything with your adopted dog is going pretty much according to plan. What about any problems that may crop up? Health matters should have been caught during your important first visit to the veterinarian, but you could run into some other unexpected difficulties.

Let's say, for example, that you don't have children and you never thought about how the dog would react to other people's children. When the kids next door come to say hello to your new dog, you'll find out how he feels. If he likes them, and they're old enough and are well behaved, fine. If Barney doesn't care for kids, the best you can hope is that—with your understanding and firm training—he will learn to tolerate them, always with you standing right there to supervise. Don't expect him ever to do better than that, because you have no idea why he dislikes children. He may have good reason to mistrust them. Teaching Barney to be tolerant of them in your presence is your goal. It will be your responsibility never to leave this dog where he will encounter children when he is not with you, and to always keep him on his leash when children are or may be around.

How Barney reacts to people and other dogs will be observed, and most of the problems overcome, in obedience classes. When meeting people and dogs on the street, it's up to you to handle the situation the same way that you learned and practiced in class. Barney learns that there is only one way to do things: your way. Have him "Sit" if you stop to chat, or else "Heel" as you walk on by. You can teach him "On by" as a command for him to mind his own business. (Keep very small treats in your pocket for a quick special reward when he gets it right.)

Chewing

Destructive chewing is another problem that you may not know about before-hand. It is definitely not seen in a kennel at the dog pound because there's nothing in there for him to chew. If your new dog was being fostered by a rescuer, he may not have exhibited this behavior in the foster home. To find out if he's a chewer, and to effectively extinguish his chewing if he is, every member of the family has to keep an eye on where the dog is and what he is doing. This rule applies whether Barney is a ten-week-old pup or a ten-year-old senior citizen. At the first sign that he's about to do something he shouldn't, give him a warn-ing "uh-uh" (or "aagh"), followed by a distraction. Toss him a toy. Ask him to "Sit." Always be sure that he's safely confined when no one is around, and that his safe area does not contain any items that you do not want him to chew.

If he seems to take a liking to certain items in the home, such as chair legs or your running shoes, spray a bitter chew-deterrent prod-uct (from your pet store) on these items. It tastes horrible! One lick says, "No!" without your having to say a word!

Separation Anxiety

Separation anxiety is most often brought on by those long farewells that we discussed previously. If Barney panics when you get ready to leave, the behavior could have begun with his previous owners, or with something you will never know about. A good way to help him overcome his anxiety is by a method called "saturation."

Go through all of your normal everyday preparations for leaving. Make no reaction—no eye contact, no verbal response—to any pawing or whining. Say your quick goodbye and go out the door. Return two minutes later, as if you'd forgotten something, with no fancy greeting. Just tell Barney he's a good dog as you say, "See you!" and leave again. Replay this scene over and over.

When you leave, don't stand outside the door because Barney will know you are there...remember that super scent sense! If you generally would leave the house by car, get in the car and drive around the corner. The radio you left on may not be loud enough to cover up your footsteps, so if you usually walk, walk far enough to be out of sight.

If you hear fussing as you return, don't acknowledge the dog at all. Stay for a moment and leave. Vary the length of time that you

Rescued Shiba Inu Sushi's owners have set forth boundaries in their home for her safety and good behavior.

As Basset Hugh knows, the way to avoid chewing problems from the start is by making sure that the dog has plenty of chew toys and encouraging him to use them.

stay away, building it up gradually until you can stay away for 30 minutes or so at a time. Do this over and over and over again. (You'll feel saturated, too!)

Keep all of your comings and goings casual, with just a couple of words, no pats. If there is more than one family member, share the comings and goings. It could easily take a week or more before the dog feels he can trust

someone to come back and until you can stay away for a couple of hours. And if you can't seem to get the dog over his anxiety, seek professional help.

Other Problems

Dogs are individuals, and they can come up with some very individual problems that the rescue volunteers were not told about and did not encounter during their evaluation. The volunteers are there to help, but some issues may require the talents of a professional trainer or behaviorist. Temperament problems fall into this area. If your obedience instructor cannot help with a problem, he (or your vet) should be able to recommend a behaviorist who can. The important thing is to get help as quickly as possible. The more you delay, the harder it will be to resolve the problem.

If Barney came from a shelter, it's possible that he was left there because of behavioral problems. Or, of course, the behavior may not have been a problem in his previous home, only in yours. Very few perfect pets turn up in shelters, but that's not to say most of them can't be turned into ideal pets with your help.

Some unwanted behavior is tied merely to a lack of stimulating exercise. Tossing a ball may be fun sometimes, but after a while it's boring to the dog. Taking him for an occasional ride in the car to do something different like a walk in the woods, a park or anywhere that's not an everyday place offers both mental and physical diversion.

Sometimes all a dog needs is a little brainy activity in his life to make him more cooperative. There are many breed-specific, all-breed and mixed-breed activities to consider that will brighten up any dog's life, among them agility, rally obedience, many forms of hunting, lure coursing, sledding, water events, earthdog trials and therapy visits to people in need of a little doggie loving. You get the idea. Anything you can do, a dog can do better!

IF ALL ELSE FAILS

Facing failure is not the happiest of topics, but by understanding why dog adoptions do fail, how you can prevent failure from happening and what you can and should do if it does happen, you'll be able to handle it.

A dog adoption can fail because you acted in haste. Your friend had to find his dog a home quickly and you, being the helpful dog-loving person that you are, offered your home without giving it some careful thought. Now you are stuck with a really nice dog, but one that doesn't

Shiba Inu Mandee knows that her chew toys are the only things she's supposed to sink her teeth into.

furniture and not interfere much with your daily life. Impossible! You may have thought your kids would take complete care of him. Dream on, dear parent!

However, even if you were completely realistic about most of the changes that occur when you add a dog to your life, you may not have been prepared for the length of time it takes for some dogs to adjust to a new home and family. If you really do like the dog and are keen to have it work out, give him an extended royal welcome. If the dog came with bed, bowl and biscuits, be sure you also got an agreement, signed by both you and the previous owner, turning the dog over to you. Yes, even between friends, legal ownership of a dog must be in writing.

fit your home or your lifestyle. These things happen. You took him on with the best of intentions and now you're stuck! What to do? There are several ways to solve the problem so that you and the dog are both winners.

First, be sure you have given yourself and the dog a fair chance at making a go of it. You may have expected the dog to simply take his place among your

The neighbor's dog may have been fine to have over for an occasional visit, but now he seems enormous when he's in your house all day or, in the other extreme, is under your feet. Perhaps your friend was at home all day and you work all day. (Most dogs do adjust to that change of routine once they feel secure and trust you to return.) Maybe this is a dog with behavioral problems you can't manage. No matter what the situation, if you've given it an honest try and can't cope any longer, the dog will have to undergo yet another change.

In fairness to everyone, especially the dog, first contact the previous owner to discuss the problems and to present your final decision in the matter. Don't raise his hopes by pretending you'll give it more time if you really know deep down you can't. Your friend may suddenly be able to take the dog back and would be heartbroken to hear that you had given him away. Or your friend may know of someone else who is interested in taking the dog. Whichever way you look at it, the previous owner should have first refusal.

If the owner cannot take the dog back and the dog is a purebred, you may have a place to turn for help. As

THE MOST DIFFICULT DECISION

If all else fails, your final choice is the most difficult one. If you can't keep the dog because you have not been able to curb his aggression, even after working with a professional, or if he has serious health problems and you've discussed all options with your veterinarian, then you must face reality and make a decision.

The kindest thing you can do for the dog is to take him to the veterinarian to be humanely put to sleep with you by his side. It goes without saying that this is the most difficult decision for any pet owner to make, but think only of the dog. How much kinder to have you beside him than to drop him off at the pound—like a coat left at the cleaners—while you walk out the door. After which, some complete stranger will take him into a strange room to administer an injection to a dog that is now terrified.

Doing the right thing is not always easy, but in this case, you'll feel better having done all you could to make a difficult situation easier for the dog.

we've noted previously, if the dog came directly a from a breed rescue, there is no question: the dog goes back to breed rescue. Likewise, if the dog came from a breeder, he goes back to that breeder.

The dog's veterinarian may know of a good home for him. There may even be a bulletin board in the vet's office where you can post a photo of the dog and a brief description of his needs and characteristics. You might look for a good rescue group or private no-kill shelter in your area where the dog would be properly looked after until the right home is found for him. You may be asked to make a donation, but you'll be assured that the dog will have good care.

If all of these suggestions lead to dead ends, you could put an ad in your local paper as a last resort. However, this is not a good idea if you live in a metropolitan area. And never use the phrase "Free to a good home." No matter where you live, you could be swamped with totally inappropriate replies. In a local ad you can specify the needs of the dog, such as "good for working couple with no kids," "loves to be with children" or "enjoys long walks." Be prepared to question thoroughly those who reply to your ad, and get references. You'll want to be as sure as possible that they meet the requirements of responsible dog ownership. Be prepared to be honest as to why you are putting this dog up for adoption. If the dog needs professional training that you can't afford, say so. And, finally, there's the matter of signing the dog over once again to new owners.

YOUR PROMISE TO YOUR RESCUED DOG

We've seen how many ways there are for dogs to become rescued, rehomed or adopted, and there are many caring people who really want to become responsible dog owners. It only works, however, if you take on the dog, and the job, with your eyes wide open to all that is involved.

Your promise of responsibility involves in-depth planning before getting the dog. It involves feeding, grooming and providing medical care (the latter involves neutering or spaying, although in almost every case this will be done before the dog comes home with you). It involves obedience training and teaching the dog about your home and your way of life. It involves playtime, fun, physical and mental exercise. It involves patience. And it involves adding all of these things up and multiplying by the next 10 to 15 years, depending on your dog's age. So it definitely involves commitment.

It's worth every minute and every penny! Nothing compares with the companionship, the laughter (dogs provide us with lots of it) and the steadfast devotion of our dog. Dogs never criticize, always forgive and seem to know when we need a friendly comforting paw or nuzzle. It has been said that no one appreciates the very special genius of your conversation as a dog does. Ask any dog owner and he'll agree. We all talk to our dogs.

Enjoy the new member of your family—and take very good care of him, no matter how he happened to come into your life.

Of course training is essential, but plenty of love is necessary to help a rescue dog settle into and feel comfortable in a new home and family.

INDEX